"Too often, Christians think narrowly about ~~...~~ saying 'Christ died for our sins' exhausts the gospel. Jonty Rhodes gives us a more full-orbed view of the work of Christ, taking us back to classical formulations of Christ's threefold office (prophet, priest, and king) and twofold state (humiliation and exaltation). *Man of Sorrows, King of Glory* is theologically rich while remaining accessible and devotional. This edifying book will help Christians understand Jesus more fully and love him more deeply."

Gavin Ortlund, Senior Pastor, First Baptist Church of Ojai; author, *Finding the Right Hills to Die On*

"As soon as we begin to speak of Jesus, we're doing the work of theology. This book provides sound teaching for that task, exploring the person and work of Christ with a fresh sense of wonder. *Man of Sorrows, King of Glory* is rich without being dense, theological without being stuffy, and corrective without being combative."

Nancy Guthrie, Bible teacher; author, *Even Better than Eden*

"This book is full of biblical insight and draws on a rich stock of historic Reformed theologians. In *Man of Sorrows, King of Glory*, we move from Adam to the new creation and see how in Christ's exaltation he becomes the human king the world has been awaiting. Jonty Rhodes shows that the death and resurrection of Jesus have so much more importance for Christians than we usually recognize."

Simon Gathercole, Professor of New Testament and Early Christianity, University of Cambridge

"Pastor Jonty Rhodes's words comfort us that our dear Savior, Jesus Christ, is both immanently sympathetic and transcendently sovereign. This book helps inform us how understanding Christ's threefold office as our prophet who teaches us, our priest who mediates for us, and our king who rules over us makes a daily difference."

Karen Hodge, Coordinator of CDM Women's Ministries, Presbyterian Church in America; coauthor, *Transformed*

"Some people think that being Reformed means believing in the five *solas* of the Reformation or the five points of Calvinism. In his book *Man of Sorrows, King of Glory*, Jonty Rhodes shows us that the Reformed faith is deeper and broader, as he invites us to look at the person and work of Christ from the perspective of his twofold state (humiliation and exaltation) and threefold office (prophet, priest, and king) set within the drama of the relationship between Father and Son. This book helps us understand the gospel through new eyes as we see the rich structures that undergird Reformed theology. I hope all Christian ministers will encourage every church member to read it!"

Jonny Gibson, Associate Professor of Old Testament, Westminster Theological Seminary

"Rare are the books that make forgotten theology accessible. Rarer still are those that do so while retaining their sense of wonder. In *Man of Sorrows, King of Glory*, we dive deep into ancient truths concerning the person and work of the Lord Jesus Christ. Combining biblical insight with devotional application, this book is one to read slowly, prayerfully, and joyfully. And as we do so, we can't fail to find ourselves in awe and love and praise at the humiliation and exaltation of so great a Savior."

Dave Gobbett, Lead Minister, Highfields Church, Cardiff, Wales; Trustee, World Alive

"In this clear and engaging study of, and meditation on, our Lord's threefold office, Jonty Rhodes reaches beyond the academic community to hold out great encouragement to the contemporary church. The theological significance and pastoral relevance of understanding Christ as our prophet, priest, and king is explained and applied in this book in a way that stirs the heart to worship. Indeed, the emphasis on the ongoing nature of the Lord's work in his church today is a particular highlight of the book that will refresh how many of us think about the Christian life."

Reuben Hunter, Lead Pastor, Trinity West Church, London

Man of Sorrows, King of Glory

TRUTH FOR LIFE®

THE BIBLE-TEACHING MINISTRY OF **ALISTAIR BEGG**

The mission of Truth For Life is to teach the Bible with clarity and relevance so that unbelievers will be converted, believers will be established, and local churches will be strengthened.

Daily Program

Each day, Truth For Life distributes the Bible teaching of Alistair Begg across the U.S. and in several locations outside of the U.S. through 2,000 radio outlets. To find a radio station near you, visit **truthforlife.org/stationfinder**.

Free Teaching

The daily program, and Truth For Life's entire teaching library of over 3,000 Bible-teaching messages, can be accessed for free online at **truthforlife.org** and through Truth For Life's mobile app, which can be download for free from your app store.

At-Cost Resources

Books and audio studies from Alistair Begg are available for purchase at cost, with no markup. Visit **truthforlife.org/store**.

Where to Begin?

If you're new to Truth For Life and would like to know where to begin listening and learning, find starting point suggestions at **truthforlife.org/firststep**. For a full list of ways to connect with Truth For Life, visit **truthforlife.org/subscribe**.

Contact Truth For Life

P.O. Box 398000 Cleveland, Ohio 44139
phone 1 (888) 588-7884   **email** letters@truthforlife.org
truthforlife.org

Man of Sorrows, King of Glory

What the Humiliation and Exaltation of Jesus Mean for Us

Jonty Rhodes

CROSSWAY®

WHEATON, ILLINOIS

Cover design: Darren Welch

First printing 2021

Printed in the United States of America

Unless otherwise indicated, Scripture quotations are from the ESV® Bible (The Holy Bible, English Standard Version®), copyright © 2001 by Crossway, a publishing ministry of Good News Publishers. Used by permission. All rights reserved.

Scripture quotations marked (NIV) are taken from the Holy Bible, New International Version®, NIV®. Copyright © 1973, 1978, 1984, 2011 by Biblica, Inc.™ Used by permission of Zondervan. All rights reserved worldwide. www.zondervan.com. The "NIV" and "New International Version" are trademarks registered in the United States Patent and Trademark Office by Biblica, Inc.™

All emphases in Scripture quotations have been added by the author.

Trade paperback ISBN: 978-1-4335-7170-1
ePub ISBN: 978-1-4335-7173-2
PDF ISBN: 978-1-4335-7171-8
Mobipocket ISBN: 978-1-4335-7172-5

Library of Congress Cataloging-in-Publication Data

Names: Rhodes, Jonty (Clergy), author.
Title: Man of sorrows, King of glory : what the humiliation and exaltation of Jesus mean for us / Jonty Rhodes.
Description: Wheaton, Illinois : Crossway, [2021] | Includes bibliographical references and index.
Identifiers: LCCN 2020026187 (print) | LCCN 2020026188 (ebook) | ISBN 9781433571701 (trade paperback) | ISBN 9781433571718 (pdf) | ISBN 9781433571725 (mobi) | ISBN 9781433571732 (epub)
Subjects: LCSH: Jesus Christ—Humiliation. | Jesus Christ—Exaltation. | Jesus Christ—Person and offices.
Classification: LCC BT222 .R46 2021 (print) | LCC BT222 (ebook) | DDC 232/.1—dc23
LC record available at https://lccn.loc.gov/2020026187
LC ebook record available at https://lccn.loc.gov/2020026188

Crossway is a publishing ministry of Good News Publishers.

BP		32	31	30	29	28	27	26	25	24	23	22
14	13	12	11	10	9	8	7	6	5	4	3	2

For Charlotte, Mathilda, Ottilie, and Henry:
May Christ the prophet grant you sight,
Christ the priest cleanse you,
Christ the king conquer and subdue all your enemies.

Contents

PART 3: TO THE FATHER'S RIGHT HAND
CHRIST'S EXALTATION

Man of Sorrows! what a name
For the Son of God, who came
Ruined sinners to reclaim:
Hallelujah! what a Savior!

Bearing shame and scoffing rude,
In my place condemned he stood,
Sealed my pardon with his blood:
Hallelujah! what a Savior!

Guilty, vile, and helpless, we;
Spotless Lamb of God was he;
Full atonement! can it be?
Hallelujah! what a Savior!

Lifted up was he to die,
"It is finished!" was his cry:
Now in heav'n exalted high:
Hallelujah! what a Savior!

When he comes, our glorious King,
All his ransomed home to bring,
Then anew this song we'll sing:
Hallelujah! what a Savior!

PHILIP BLISS, 1875

Written . . . shortly before his death, this was the last hymn
I heard Mr. Bliss sing. . . . When Mr. Moody and I were in
Paris, holding meetings in the old church which Napoleon

had granted to the Evangelicals, I frequently sang this hymn as a solo, asking the congregation to join in the single phrase, "Hallelujah, what a Saviour," which they did with splendid effect. It is said that the word "Hallelujah" is the same in all languages. It seems as though God had prepared it for the great jubilee of heaven, when all his children shall have been gathered home to sing "Hallelujah to the Lamb!"

IRA D. SANKEY

PART 1

———————

THE JOURNEY OF
THE SON OF GOD

1

Man of Sorrows! What a Name

The Whole Christ and the Whole Cross

WHAT HAS JESUS DONE FOR YOU? Ask that question in any Bible-honoring church, and you'll likely hear the same answer: "He died for me." Christians are known as people of the cross, and rightly so. The cross stands at the center of the good news of salvation for sinners. Hence the apostle Paul's resolution in ministering to the Corinthians, "to know nothing among you except Jesus Christ and him crucified" (1 Cor. 2:2).

And so we strive to be gospel-centered parents, cross-centered preachers, Christ-centered worshipers. All this is well and good: the cross *is* at the heart of the gospel. But there are two pitfalls we would do well to avoid.

The Danger of a Disconnected Cross

To say the cross is at the center of Christ's work immediately implies that there's a wider picture; a broader canvas that *has* a center. My children recently had to study John Constable's painting *The*

Hay Wain. In the middle of the canvas, resting in a gently flowing river, is the hay wain itself (*wain* being an old English word for a wagon). But to fully appreciate this centerpiece, you also need to see the setting: the Suffolk meadows in the background, the dog playing in the shallows, the rowboat tucked in the rushes. So too the cross. The cross must not become detached from the resurrection, the ascension, or any other event in Christ's life. We may be able to answer the question "Why did Jesus die for you?" But why did he rise? Why was he buried? Why was he circumcised?

Does it even matter? Yes, I suggest it does. God has spoken about all these things in his word, and God doesn't waste his breath. All the events of Christ's life are part of his saving work: he was buried *for us*, he was circumcised *for us*, he was baptized *for us*. Each has something to teach us.

The cross connects not just to every other event in Christ's life but to every aspect of his ministry. Historically, this ministry has been viewed through the lens of Christ's threefold office. Jesus is our prophet, priest, and king. We'll explore these three aspects of Christ's office in the chapters ahead, but for now I'm simply claiming that the cross relates to each one. Of course the cross is about Christ's priestly ministry: we readily see how he is the perfect sacrifice for sin. As those outside (and sadly sometimes inside) the church attack the view that Jesus was bearing the wrath of God at our sin, we've become justifiably ferocious in our defense of what is known as penal-substitutionary atonement. Yet penal substitution doesn't exhaust the significance of Golgotha. Without it, as I'll argue later, nothing else makes sense. But we need to connect the cross to Christ's prophetic and kingly work too. The cross is Christ's pulpit and throne as well as altar. As Gavin Ortlund puts it, "a rigorous 'cross-centeredness,' rightly understood, need not entail a focus on the cross instead of other aspects of salvation—but rather the cross at their center, as in a great spider web."[1]

The Danger of a Disconnected Christ

In stitching the cross back into the work of Christ as prophet, priest, and king, and in reattaching it to the other events recorded in the Gospels, our work is only half done. If we're to see the whole canvas, we need to ask not just what Jesus has done for us but what he's doing now. Again, those who've gone before us are on hand to help. Alongside Christ's threefold office, they also speak of Christ's two states: the state of humiliation and the state of exaltation. These two states describe Jesus's journey. His humiliation begins at the incarnation and takes him through to his burial. His exaltation begins at his resurrection and ends—well, in one sense, never!

Question 23 of the Westminster Shorter Catechism gives a concise summary of an understanding of Christ's work that emphasizes his twofold state and threefold office:

Q. What offices does Christ execute as our redeemer?
A. Christ, as our redeemer, executes the offices of a prophet, of a priest, and of a king, both in his estate of humiliation and exaltation.[2]

---

1 Gavin Ortlund, "'The Voice of His Blood': Christ's Intercession in the Thought of Stephen Charnock," *Themelios* 38, no. 3 (2013): 375–89, https://www.thegospelcoalition.org/themelios/article/the-voice-of-his-blood-christs-intercession-in-the-thought-of-stephen-charn/.
2 Westminster Shorter Catechism, Orthodox Presbyterian Church, https://www.opc.org/sc.html. I have lightly modernized the language of the Westminster Standards throughout the book.

In a right desire to be cross centered, it's possible that we've fallen into the trap of only ever speaking about Christ in his humiliation and neglecting his ongoing work in his state of exaltation. Perhaps without noticing, we begin to preach a disconnected Christ. "Jesus was a great Savior; he was the Messiah; he was God's Son come to earth." What's the problem here? Not the nouns but the verbs—or, to be more precise, the tenses. It's not just that Jesus *was* our Savior; he *remains* so today. He is just as active as Messiah now as he was two thousand years ago in Jerusalem.

Think of the last time you heard a sermon. What was going on? Whose voice were you hearing? Only the pastor's, as he faithfully expounded God's word? Disconnect Jesus from his ongoing work, and that's all you're left with: one man telling others about a distant third party. It's far more wonderful to realize that Christ himself was speaking to you in his ongoing work as prophet.

Or think of mission. It's so easy to slip into the mindset that says Jesus died for our sins, retired to heaven, and left us with the job of gathering a people for him. Then we remember his own words: "*I* will build my church, and the gates of hell shall not prevail against it" (Matt. 16:18). "I will." It is Jesus who is building, not us. He is still active as a conquering king. We preach the parable of the lost sheep and drive toward a rousing exhortation to be like Jesus and go and find those lost sheep. But subtly, we've shifted the focus from Jesus to us. The shepherd in the parable becomes first and foremost an example for us to follow rather than a reminder of the love of Christ—which, of course, we should then try to imitate but only in a secondary sense. We must not disconnect Christ from his ongoing ministry today. If we do, someone will have to pick up the work, and that usually leads to burdened pastors and guilt-laden sheep.

But does the Bible really present Jesus as having this threefold office in a twofold state, or is this just a case of "theologians at play"? Let's turn to the story and see the patterns unfold.

Back to the Beginning

A man was in a garden. He was a good man. Holy. Happy. Healthy.

But he was alone, and his Father saw it. So the Father gently put the man to sleep and pierced his side. From the flesh and bone of the man came a bride, and when the man awoke and saw her, he sang for joy.

But there was a serpent in the grass. The serpent was full of poison and, unable to attack the almighty Father, struck at the bride instead. The bride was in danger, but the man was there. The mighty king commissioned to protect her. The faithful prophet to warn her. The zealous priest to guard the holiness of his beloved and her sanctuary. It was time to crush the serpent's head.

The man stayed still. The man stayed silent. His sword stayed sheathed.

The serpent struck. The bride fell.

So begins the story of the world . . .

Introducing Adam

That's a story I imagine you recognize, but it's not a story originally written for you. Jesus tells us it's a story written by Moses, so it's a story whose first readers were Israelites. The Israelites lived in a very different world from ours, a world of Pharaohs and pyramids;

of snakes and deserts; and, most significantly for our purposes, of prophets, priests, and kings.

These were the three roles given to Adam in the garden, as any Israelite would immediately have noticed. None of those three words (*prophet*, *priest*, or *king*) is used in Genesis 1–2, but that doesn't mean the concepts aren't there. We're used to picking up messages from stories without a narrator needing constantly to interrupt to explain. Any child upon hearing, "Rollo put on his crown, gathered his robes, and settled into his throne," knows straightaway that Rollo is a king. For that matter, any Christian can read Genesis 3 and know that we're seeing the origin of sin, though none of the Bible's words for "sin" are used.

So let's meet Adam the prophet, priest, and king.

Adam the King

Adam's kingly office is perhaps the easiest to see:

> Then God said, "Let us make man in our image, after our likeness. And let them have dominion over the fish of the sea and over the birds of the heavens and over the livestock and over all the earth and over every creeping thing that creeps on the earth." (Gen. 1:26)

Adam has dominion, or rule, over the earth. Only God stands above him. As the firstborn of all creation, Adam was to rule in the image of his gracious heavenly Father, overseeing the extension of his kingdom from shore to shore, as he worked and developed God's world.

Adam the Prophet

Prophets in the Bible speak God's words to God's people. And in the garden Adam receives just this task:

> The LORD God took the man and put him in the garden of Eden to work it and keep it. And the LORD God commanded the man, saying, "You may surely eat of every tree of the garden, but of the tree of the knowledge of good and evil you shall not eat, for in the day that you eat of it you shall surely die." (Gen. 2:15–17)

Why does this command establish Adam as the first prophet? Notice when it comes: before God has made the woman. At this stage Adam is alone. How is Eve (as she is later named) to know to avoid the fruit of the tree of the knowledge of good and evil? By Adam telling her. The story is very carefully written to make it clear that Adam alone receives this knowledge directly from God. This is part of the reason why, ultimately, Adam rather than Eve bears final responsibility for the fall. Adam is a prophet whose duty is to faithfully pass on God's holy word to his bride. He must reveal God's will to God's people.

Adam the Priest

Of all the offices, the priestly office is the one we're most likely to miss, lacking, as we do, the language and customs of the original Israelite readers. But look again at Genesis 2:15. Adam is to "work" and "keep" the garden in Eden. What does this involve? On its own we might assume that working was simply gardening: Adam is to plant seeds, water crops, take in the harvest. And no doubt, he did just that—or would have done had he not rebelled. But the Hebrew word is used elsewhere in a more expansive sense to mean worship or service of God: it has "temple" connotations. And what about "keep"? What does it mean for Adam to "keep" the garden? The sense here is to guard—to keep safe, we might say.

Significantly, later in the writings of Moses, these two words ("work" [or "minister," ESV] and "keep") are paired again to describe the work of the Levites, the priestly tribe, in guarding and serving God in the tabernacle (Num. 3:7–8). In fact, G. K. Beale has shown that the whole description of the garden is meant to make us think of the tabernacle or temple.[3] At the simplest level, a temple is where God meets his people, and it is in the garden that God comes to meet Adam and Eve. There are other, subtler clues too. The entrance to the garden was on the east; so was the entrance to the tabernacle. The candlestick in the temple was shaped like a tree, reminiscent of the trees of the garden. Also, Solomon's temple was decorated all over with carvings of flowers and trees (1 Kings 6). And just as the garden was eventually guarded by two cherubim, so the temple curtain that kept men from coming back into God's Holy Place had cherubim woven into it. It seems that both Adam's job description and his place of work are meant to make us think of him as a priest.

In the Bible, priestly work is all about holiness and worship. Later this will involve offering sacrifices for sin, to cleanse what

---

3 For a fuller description of the links between Eden and the temple, see G. K. Beale, *The Temple and the Church's Mission: A Biblical Theology of the Dwelling Place of God*, New Studies in Biblical Theology 17 (Downers Grove, IL: InterVarsity Press, 2004). For a shorter introduction, see G. K. Beale and Mitchell Kim, *God Dwells among Us: Expanding Eden to the Ends of the Earth* (Nottingham, UK: Inter-Varsity Press, 2014).

has become dirty. But for Adam, before mankind rebels, his chief duty is to protect the holiness of paradise—and Eve—from Satan, leading them in joyful thanksgiving to God. Already he is the appointed guardian of God's people, the rescuer from Satanic threat.

So Adam is prophet, priest, and king. And why? For the blessing of his bride. Don't miss this: all three roles make sense only in relation to someone else. A prophet on his own isn't much use. Neither is a king with no one to rule or a priest with no one to guard and protect. No, Adam was given these roles for the sake of others. Initially, this is Eve, but in time his responsibility would also be to their descendants. Adam was to be head of the church and therefore prophet, priest, and king for all God's people. After all, as Paul tells us, Eve was a picture of the church, the bride of Christ (Eph. 5).

The Serpent Strikes

Suddenly, it all goes wrong. Satan, the serpent, slides into paradise, and Adam fails to act. As prophet, Adam should have spoken up and led Eve to the truth when Satan started to cast doubt on God's word. As king, Adam should have exercised his rule over all creatures and conquered the snake. As priest, Adam ought to have crushed the serpent's head and protected the holiness of both his bride and his garden-temple. But instead—standing by Eve's side (Gen. 3:6)—he watched as she reached out and plucked sin and misery from the tree. Indeed, he joined her in rebellion, a false prophet, a defeated king, an unclean priest.

And so sin entered the world. Humanity became blind to the truth about God, ignorant of his glory and goodness. We became guilty and unclean, stained by the corruption of sin, enslaved to Satan and our own distorted passions. That's why a second Adam was needed: a true prophet to open our eyes, a priest to cleanse us from sin, and a king to conquer death and the devil on our behalf. In short: a Messiah.

Short-Term Saviors: The Many Messiahs

As the story of the Old Testament unfolds, God sends a series of people to fill these roles. Prophets preach, priests sacrifice, kings rule. Each, in their limited way, is a messiah, a minichrist. *Messiah* is the Hebrew word for "anointed," and *Christ* is its Greek equivalent. Prophets, priests, and kings all had oil poured on their heads as a sign of their commissioning for their roles. We might say that David was "messiahed" as king in 1 Samuel 16. Aaron was "messiahed" as priest in Leviticus 8. Elijah was to "messiah" Elisha as prophet in 1 Kings 19 (cf. 1 Chron. 16:22).

None, however, can deal fully and finally with the problem of sin. For that we need one greater than all the prophets, priests, and kings of the Old Testament combined.

Jesus Messiah

As we come to the New Testament, the Holy Spirit takes the categories of prophet, priest, and king that he has already established in Israel's history and weaves them together to give a glorious portrait of Jesus the Messiah. The official anointing of Jesus comes at his baptism, where he is anointed—"messiahed"—not with oil but with the Holy Spirit, who descends on him in the form of a dove. Although Jesus has, of course, been filled with the Spirit since his conception (Luke 1:35), this anointing marks his official commissioning as God's Messiah at the start of his public ministry. Shortly afterward, he enters a synagogue and, reading from Isaiah, announces,

> The Spirit of the Lord is upon me,
>   because he has anointed me. (Luke 4:18)

He is the truly Spirit-anointed Christ, gathering the offices of prophet, priest, and king up into his own person. This is why we've spoken of one threefold office rather than three offices. Jesus's office is that of Messiah or Redeemer. He fulfills that calling in three ways: as prophet, priest, and king.

Unsurprisingly, therefore, Jesus is explicitly called a prophet, a priest, and a king at various points in the New Testament, as we'll see. In Matthew 12, he claims to be greater than Jonah the prophet, Solomon the king, and the temple itself. At other times, the allusions are subtler. Matthew's Gospel begins by claiming that Jesus is the son of David, listing his family tree, replete with Israel's kings, and it ends with Jesus claiming "all authority in heaven and on earth" (Matt. 28:18). Mark begins with quotations from two Old Testament prophets and moves straight to the ministry of John the Baptist, the last prophet before Christ. It ends with Mary and the other women being sent to "go, tell" of Jesus's resurrection (Mark 16:7). And Luke begins and ends in the temple, the priestly zone: Zechariah the priest receiving an angelic visit in chapter 1 and Christ blessing the disciples, arms aloft like Aaron, before they return to worship God back in his temple in chapter 24. Christ the anointed one is a greater prophet, priest, and king.

The Heidelberg Catechism spells this out:

Q. 31. Why is he called "Christ," meaning "anointed"?
A. Because he has been ordained by God the Father
   and has been anointed with the Holy Spirit
      to be
      our chief prophet and teacher
         who perfectly reveals to us
         the secret counsel and will of God for our deliverance;
      our only high priest
         who has set us free by the one sacrifice of his body,
         and who continually pleads our cause with the Father;
      and our eternal king
         who governs us by his Word and Spirit,
         and who guards us and keeps us
         in the freedom he has won for us.[4]

God the Messiah?

Back to Genesis. Adam and Eve have taken the fruit, and the serpent has triumphed. Then God enters the scene. First, he calls to gather his wayward children and to promise that one day Satan will be crushed. Then he punishes the snake, demonstrating his complete authority over him. Finally, he clothes the man and the woman with animal skins: blood has been shed that they might be clothed, their shame covered. God has stepped in as prophet, priest, and king.

Yet these were roles that Adam was meant to fulfill, and it is one of Eve's sons, God announces, who will ultimately crush the ser-

4 *The Heidelberg Catechism* (Grand Rapids, MI: Faith Alive, 1988), 21.

pent's head. So who would this Messiah be? Already, it seems, we're getting a hint that he would need to be both God and man. Some have held that any time God appears in the Old Testament, it is God the Son whom we should understand to be present—and that therefore it is the Son whom we hear in Genesis 3, already acting in his threefold office. Whatever we make of this, it's certainly the case that the Son was Redeemer before he became man: he functioned as mediator from the fall onward. As Geerhardus Vos puts it, "Prophets, priests, and kings in Israel were not only shadows or types but also messengers and representatives of the great antitype. They derived their official authority from the person Himself whom they as office bearers proclaimed in a shadowy fashion."[5] The Old Testament system wasn't just a visual aid. Although in itself it was utterly powerless to deliver salvation, Christ was already active through it, giving the grace to his people that he would win for them when finally he came to earth.

So before we look at the work of Christ, we must be clear on his identity. In fact, we must be careful not to separate the subjects of his person and work too sharply. Even those Christians who hold the Bible in the highest regard can fall into the trap of thinking of salvation as a series of gifts given by Jesus but somehow separate from him.

J. I. Packer cautions us:

Some Christians seem to prefer the epistles as if this were a mark of growing up spiritually; but really this attitude is a very

---

5 Geerhardus Vos, *Reformed Dogmatics*, vol. 3, *Christology*, trans. and ed. Richard B. Gaffin Jr. (Bellingham, WA: Lexham, 2014), 90.

bad sign, suggesting that we are more interested in theological notions than in fellowship with the Lord Jesus in person.[6]

Of course, good theology itself is not the problem, because good theology leads us to the person of Jesus. In fact, every benefit of our salvation is found in him. He is not a divine Father Christmas, dispensing gifts of salvation; he *is* the gift.

As Stephen Charnock writes, "There is something in Christ more excellent and comely than the office of a Saviour; the greatness of his person is more excellent, than the salvation procured by his death."[7]

We must not separate Christ from the gospel, still less prize the gifts above the giver. Consider one final quotation, from the Puritan Samuel Rutherford, who wrote these extraordinary words to Lady Kilconquhar:

Put the beauty of ten thousand thousand worlds of paradises like the garden of Eden in one.

Put all trees, all flowers, all smells, all colours, all tastes, all joys, all sweetness, all loveliness in one. O, what a fair and excellent thing that would be! And yet it would be less to that fair and dearest Well-Beloved Christ, than one drop of rain to the whole seas, rivers, lakes, and fountains of ten thousand earths.[8]

6 J. I. Packer, *Keep in Step with the Spirit: Finding Fullness in Our Walk with God*, exp. ed. (Leicester, UK: Inter-Varsity Press, 2005), 61.

7 Quoted in Mark Jones, *A Christian's Pocket Guide to Jesus Christ: An Introduction to Christology* (Fearn, Ross-shire, Scotland: Christian Focus, 2012), 3.

8 Samuel Rutherford, *Letters of Samuel Rutherford*, ed. Andrew A. Bonar (Edinburgh: Oliphant, Anderson, and Ferrier, 1891), 446 (letter 226, to the Lady Kilconquhar).

That is the invitation of the gospel. Not so much "Receive these gifts: justification, sanctification, adoption, reconciliation," but rather "Receive Christ." After all, as Jesus said in his high priestly prayer to the Father, "This is eternal life, that they know you, the only true God, and Jesus Christ whom you have sent" (John 17:3). So we turn now to think about the person of Christ, before exploring his threefold office in his two states of humiliation and exaltation.

2

For the Son of God, Who Came

The Person of Christ

CHRISTIANS HAVE ALWAYS BELIEVED that Jesus is both God and man. The traditional way of putting this in more theological language is that in Christ we meet one person in two natures. The one person is the Son of God, the second person of the Trinity. The two natures are his fully divine nature (in which he always existed) and, from the incarnation onward, his fully human nature. Question 35 of the Heidelberg Catechism gives a great summary:

> Q. 35. What does it mean that he "was conceived by the Holy Spirit and born of the virgin Mary"?
> A. That the eternal Son of God,
>> who is and remains
>> true and eternal God,
> took to himself,
>> through the working of the Holy Spirit,
>> from the flesh and blood of the virgin Mary,

a truly human nature
> so that he might also become David's true descendant,
> like his brothers in every way
>> except for sin.[1]

Let's dig a little deeper.

One Person

When you ask the question "Who is Jesus?" the fundamental answer is that he is God the Son. Like God the Father and God the Holy Spirit, he has always existed. He is the Creator of all things. John's Gospel begins with a striking statement:

> In the beginning was the Word, and the Word was with God, and the Word was God. (John 1:1)

As the story unfolds, Jesus will claim to be one with the Father (John 10:30), will tell Philip that "whoever has seen me has seen the Father" (John 14:9), and will accept Thomas's acclamation of him as "my Lord and my God" (John 20:28). And John's Gospel is hardly alone in presenting us with Jesus as God. Matthew introduces Christ as "Immanuel (which means, God with us)" (Matt. 1:23), Paul describes him as "the image of the invisible God" (Col. 1:15), and the author of Hebrews tells us that Jesus is "the radiance of the glory of God and the exact imprint of his nature" (Heb. 1:3). We could multiply verses almost endlessly. We could look at descriptions of Jesus

---

1   *The Heidelberg Catechism* (Grand Rapids, MI: Faith Alive, 1988), 23.

doing things that only God can do. But I suspect you're on board: Jesus is God.

The *person* in *one person, two natures* is God the Son.

Two Natures

That means, of course, that we're halfway to answering the *two natures* question. If Jesus is the Son of God, then he has a fully divine nature. Anything that is true of God is true of Jesus. God knows all things, so Jesus knows all things. God is all-powerful, so Jesus is all-powerful. God is omnipresent, so Jesus is omnipresent. The only difference between God the Father and God the Son is that one is Father and one is Son. Jesus is, to use the language of the Nicene Creed, "of one substance with the Father." Jesus is not *like* God the Father or similar to him. They are one substance—because there is only one God.

And now, perhaps, questions are beginning to stir. We remember that Jesus didn't know when he was returning, yet God knows all things. We see him asleep in the boat on the Sea of Galilee, yet we have read in the Psalms that God "will neither slumber nor sleep" (Ps. 121:4). We see Jesus getting hungry and thirsty, but God suffers neither of these weaknesses (Ps. 50:12–13). Most significant of all, we see Christ crucified, dead, and buried, but God himself is immortal, incapable of dying (1 Tim. 1:17).

At this point, various perversions of orthodox Christianity spring up and claim that this is proof that Jesus isn't really God, at least not in the truest, fullest sense. Jehovah's Witnesses, Mormons, and Christadelphians all, in different ways, deny that Christ is "of one nature" with the Father. But Christians from the earliest centuries have understood the kinds of verses above as evidence that the Son of God became man. The Jesus we meet in the Gospels, the Jesus who sits on the throne of heaven, is fully human. In addition to his divine nature, when Jesus came to earth, he took on a second nature, a human nature.

When we looked for evidence that the Bible presents Jesus as fully divine, we began with John 1:1, "The Word was God." But look how John continues: "The Word became flesh and dwelt among us" (John 1:14). And again, we can look beyond John's Gospel. Paul speaks of "the man Christ Jesus" (1 Tim. 2:5), and Hebrews tells us that since "the children share in flesh and blood, he himself likewise partook of the same things. . . . Therefore he had to be made like his brothers in every respect" (Heb. 2:14, 17). The children here are God's people. Jesus became like us in "every respect" (apart from sin, of course, Heb. 4:15), sharing our "flesh and blood." Perhaps most striking of all, Jesus refers to himself as "a man who has told you the truth that I heard from God" (John 8:40).

Jesus is really, fully human. The Son of God added to himself a human nature. Everything it means to be human is true, now, for Jesus. He didn't just "slip on a skin suit," as I once heard a preacher say. He didn't just *appear* like a man. He really is one of us.

The God-Man

The coming of the Son of God to earth is known as the incarnation. *Carnis* is Latin for flesh, so *incarnation* simply means "in flesh." This incarnation was an addition, not a subtraction: the Son didn't give up any of his divine powers when he became man. For a start, this is impossible. God does not change (Mal. 3:6; James 1:17). He is also not made up of "parts." As human beings, we're made up of arms plus legs plus brains plus souls plus . . . I won't go on. But God isn't like that. He is *simple*, to use the theological term. *Simple* here doesn't mean "easy to understand" but rather that he's not constructed of different bits like we are. God's various attributes and characteristics aren't like slices of a pizza, as if we could remove a few easily enough and still say we had a pizza left. He is one simple being; he is truly *one*. Jesus remains this one true God, never losing any of his powers: if he had given up any of his attributes when he came to earth, he would have ceased to be God.

In fact, even talking about "coming to earth" is to use picture language. Using picture language to describe God and his work is okay, of course—necessary even. But we need to recognize it for what it is, lest we draw the wrong conclusion from the picture. With regard to the Son of God leaving heaven, John Calvin writes,

> The Son of God descended from heaven in such a way that, without leaving heaven, he willed to be borne in the virgin's womb, to go about the earth, and to hang upon the cross; yet he continuously filled the world even as he had done from the beginning![2]

This is hard—impossible—to comprehend. Gavin Ortlund asks us to imagine J. R. R. Tolkien writing himself into his *Lord of the Rings* story and going on the journey to Mordor with

---

2 John Calvin, *Institutes of the Christian Religion*, ed. John T. McNeill, trans. Ford Lewis Battles, Library of Christian Classics (Louisville: Westminster John Knox, 1960), 806 (2.18.4).

Frodo. Would Tolkien therefore cease to be in Oxford? Would his Oxford existence be changed in any way by his appearance in the book, his creation? No. As Ortlund concedes, this could, like any illustration, be pushed in an unhelpful direction, but it perhaps helps us glimpse something of how Jesus could remain what he was while also taking on flesh in the realm of creation.[3]

It's worth noting that some have tried to claim that in becoming man, Jesus did give up some of his more spectacular powers. Often this is based on a rather unhelpful reading of Philippians 2:7, which in some translations tells us that Jesus "emptied himself."

The Greek word for "empty," *kenoō*, has given its name to what's known as *kenosis theory*. Those who hold to it teach that while Jesus retained his mercy, love, wisdom, kindness, and so on, he emptied himself of his omnipotence, his omnipresence, and his omniscience. Some of the more extreme advocates of this idea even claim that this is why Jesus makes (what they view as) mistakes, such as claiming that Moses wrote Genesis.

But Paul's point in Philippians is not that Jesus emptied himself of certain abilities, chopping off bits as he came to earth. If we read the verse carefully, we see that the text never mentions any contents that are "emptied"; we're not told that Jesus emptied himself of certain things. No, the next clause explains what this emptying means: the Lord of glory became a servant, became a man like us. In fact, in some modern translations, the verse above is helpfully translated as "made himself nothing." Jesus emptied

---

3 Gavin Ortlund, "He Lay in a Manger without Leaving Heaven," The Gospel Coalition, December 14, 2017, https://www.thegospelcoalition.org/article/he-lay-in-manger-without-leaving-heaven/.

himself by "taking," taking the form of a servant. The king threw on a beggar's cloak, concealing his true glory.

So when you think of the incarnation, think of an addition, not a subtraction. The Son of God took to himself a truly human nature. Or as one early theologian, Gregory of Nazianzus, wrote, "Remaining what he was, he became what he was not."[4] Keeping everything it means to be God, he became everything it means to be man.

The Personal Union

To return to where we began, in Jesus we meet one person (the Son of God) in two natures (divine and human). Both these natures keep all their properties; they don't change, mix together, or "balance each other out." There is, of course, great mystery here. We'll never fully comprehend what it means for Jesus to be God and man or how his two natures hold together in his one person. But we can learn to think and speak truly, if not exhaustively, about Christ.

We need to navigate a path between two opposite errors. One is to follow the path of Nestorianism, which, broadly speaking, teaches that Jesus is two persons in two natures: you have a human Jesus and a divine Jesus.[5] To counter this notion, we must remember that the Son of God didn't take to himself a human *person* but

---

4 For versions of this line, see Herman Bavinck, *The Wonderful Works of God: Instruction in the Christian Religion according to the Reformed Confession* (Glenside, PA: Westminster Seminary Press, 2019), 306; St. Gregory of Nazianzus, *On God and Christ: The Five Theological Orations and Two Letters to Cledonius*, Popular Patristics (Yonkers, NY: St. Vladimir's Seminary Press, 2002), 86.

5 Named after Nestorius, archbishop of Constantinople in the early fifth century.

a human *nature*. There is no man called Jesus of Nazareth who exists separately from the Son of God.

At the same time, we shouldn't fall into the mistake of thinking of Christ's human nature as simply his physical body, a bit like a machine brought to life by God the Son. This would be to lean toward a heresy known as Apollinarianism, the idea that the Word took the place of the mind in the man Jesus.[6] God the Son didn't replace anything in Christ's human nature, not least because nothing was missing. None of his human "agency" is lost, because God and man don't jostle for space in the universe: they exist on entirely different planes.

No, although he is one person, both Jesus's natures retain all their respective characteristics. Remember, Jesus is *truly* human. He has a human will, a human mind, and a human soul—not just a human body. This means we need to say something along the lines of John Murray's claim that in Jesus, "there are two centres of consciousness but not of self-consciousness."[7] Jesus's human mind cannot exhaust or fully comprehend his divine mind: the finite cannot contain the infinite. His divine mind knows things his human mind doesn't. But as his human mind developed and grew, he never thought himself to be anyone other than the Son of God. And his human mind, being the human mind of the Son of God, was a faithful representation, on a human level, of the divine "mind" of the Son

6 Named after Apollinaris, bishop of Laodicea in the late fourth century.

7 John Murray, *Collected Writings of John Murray*, vol. 2, *Systematic Theology* (Edinburgh: Banner of Truth, 2009), 138. See also Bavinck, who says, "The human consciousness in him, though having the same subject as the divine consciousness, only to a small degree knew that subject, that 'I.'" Herman Bavinck, *Reformed Dogmatics*, vol. 3, *Sin and Salvation in Christ*, ed. John Bolt, trans. John Vriend (Grand Rapids, MI: Baker Academic, 2006), 312.

of God. There's no "split personality" at play. How does this work out in Jesus's experience? No idea. In the beautiful phrase of Hilary of Poitiers, "What man cannot understand, God can be."[8]

This mystery is known as the hypostatic union (from the Greek word *hypostatikē*, meaning "personal"). Fully understanding it may be beyond us, but we can at least learn to speak rightly, avoid heresy, and bow in worship. So have a go. If someone were to ask you, "How is it that Jesus didn't know the date of his second coming?" what would you say? We really must not say that God the Father knows some things that God the Son doesn't. There is, after all, only one God, and both Father and Son are omniscient. So what's the answer? Well, it's that according to his human nature Jesus didn't know (just as he didn't know how many people were living in Scotland at the time or who would be the thirty-seventh president of the United States). But according to his divine nature, he knew all things, including when he would return.[9] There's

---

8   I confess that I owe this quote not to my own reading of Hilary but rather to a blog post written by my friend D. Blair Smith, "Jesus, Did You Know?," The Gospel Coalition, July 19, 2019, https://www.thegospelcoalition.org/article/jesus-know/.

9   This, of course, raises the question of why Jesus answers according to his human nature. There's debate here, but the best answer to my mind is that the Jesus we meet in the Gospels is always acting according to his human nature. He knows some things supernaturally because they are revealed to him by the Spirit, just as Elijah and other prophets knew things they couldn't have known "naturally." He doesn't choose to sometimes access his divine knowledge and sometimes not, arbitrarily. He acts consistently as Messiah, the Spirit-anointed human king. That's why there's such an emphasis in Luke in particular on Jesus being filled with the Spirit and also why he couldn't do miracles in certain places. Interestingly, both Jesus himself (Matt. 12:28) and Peter (Acts 10:38) seem to attribute at least some of Christ's miracles to the Spirit rather than to Jesus's divine nature. For more detail, see Mark Jones, *A Christian's Pocket Guide to Jesus Christ: An Introduction to Christology* (Fearn, Ross-shire, Scotland: Christian Focus, 2012); Jones also argues that this is the position of John Owen and Thomas Goodwin.

much to wonder at here. It's extraordinary to think of Jesus learning things, according to his human nature, but Luke makes clear that this is exactly what happened (Luke 2:52).

Was Wesley Right?

Before moving on, it's worth addressing how the two natures relate to each other: the question of the communication of attributes, as it's known. Take omnipresence, for example. God is present everywhere, so Jesus must be present everywhere: he's God. But does that mean his human nature becomes omnipresent? There has been debate here, even within the Protestant tradition, but the Reformed stream has answered no. The characteristics of the divine nature don't get handed over to the human nature. Jesus's human body doesn't become omnipresent; his human mind doesn't become omniscient. If they did, they would cease to be human, since by definition human beings aren't omnipresent or omniscient.

Instead, we can—and must—say that anything true of either nature is true of the person of Christ but not of the other nature (see figure 2.1).

But the Holy Spirit is happy to use shorthand. He can write of God having blood (Acts 20:28) without adding in all the detail: that this is God the Son and that the blood is part of his human, not divine, nature. It's verses like these that give rise to this doctrine of the communication of attributes. Things that are true of God the Son only in one nature can still be said to be true of his person. We can sing with Charles Wesley, "Tis mystery all, the immortal dies," without needing to squirm.[10]

---

10 From Charles Wesley's hymn "And Can It Be" (1738).

Figure 2.1   Communication of attributes

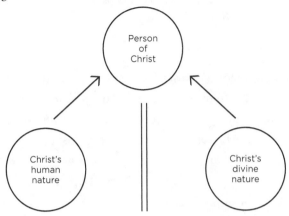

One note of caution: notice that we've been talking about Jesus doing things according to his human or divine nature. We haven't been saying, "Jesus's divine nature did this," or even worse, "God-Jesus knew everything, but Man-Jesus didn't." No, there's only one person, and natures don't do anything—only persons act. The person is always the Son of God, or Jesus, as he is named at the incarnation.[11] But Jesus acts in two natures.

The Mediator

Why does this matter? Is it just theological hairsplitting for those who like their brains scrambled? No, this is the heart of the gospel. Jesus is the Savior, and his salvation rests on him being the God-man. If Jesus is not fully divine and fully human, then

---

11 For the sake of simplicity, I've used *Jesus* throughout this chapter, though to be strictly accurate, he was given that name only at his incarnation. Mind you, Jude 5 says, "Jesus . . . saved a people out of the land of Egypt," so I'm in good company.

there is no salvation. We'll unpack this much more as we go on, but we can begin here.

Representing Man

As man, Jesus represents us. Human beings are corrupted by sin in every aspect of our being: our minds darkened, our wills enslaved to sin and Satan, our bodies cursed by decay and death. So we need a Savior who can rescue every aspect of our being.

In the early church, the nature of Christ was much debated. Although conspiracy theorists and hyped-up novels like *The Da Vinci Code* breathlessly claim that it was hundreds of years before Christians believed Jesus to be God, it was actually Christ's human nature that was more often called into question in the first centuries. But when some denied his full humanity, others spotted that if you lose this, you lose any hope of rescue. As Gregory of Nazianzus, one of the heroic defenders of orthodoxy, was fond of saying, "What is not assumed is not healed."[12] Or as his friend Gregory of Nyssa put it more poetically, the good shepherd "carries home on His shoulders the whole sheep, not its skin only."[13] To redeem our bodies, minds, souls, and emotions, Jesus had to have a truly human body, mind, even soul: yes, he was filled with the Holy Spirit, but he still had to have a human soul as we do.

12 Gregory of Nazianzus, "To Cledonius the Priest against Apollinarius," in *Christology of the Later Fathers*, ed. Edward R. Hardy, Library of Christian Classics (Philadelphia: Westminster, 1954), 218.
13 Gregory of Nyssa, *Against Eunomius*, in *A Select Library of Nicene and Post-Nicene Fathers of the Christian Church*, 2nd ser., ed. Philip Schaff and Henry Wace (New York: Charles Scribner's Sons, 1917), 5:127.

Jesus had to be one of us to live the life we should have lived and die in our place as our representative. We might be tempted to think that being sinless was the only qualification our Savior needed. But that's not the case: a sinless angel couldn't die for us. Gabriel, should he have wanted to, could no more pay for our sins than the goats and bulls of the Old Testament. He (and they) may be without sin, but they are not human, so they simply can't stand in our place. As question 14 of the Heidelberg Catechism puts it, "God will not punish another creature for what a human is guilty of."[14]

Representing God

Equally, if Jesus is not truly and fully God, then he has no right to earn and offer salvation for us. Again, Gabriel could not live and die for us, as it was not Gabriel whom we sinned against. If I steal apples from Reuben, only Reuben has the right to forgive me; Jeff turning up and announcing that he forgives me simply isn't just. If Christ were anything other than fully divine, then he would be a third party trying to rescue us from God, rather than the God we sinned against lovingly substituting himself for us. Nor could a mere man survive the curse-bearing death of the cross. In the words of George Smeaton, "A mere man could no more redeem the world as he could create the world: the Restorer of man must be the Maker of Man."[15]

---

14 *Heidelberg Catechism* (1988), 13.

15 George Smeaton, *Christ's Doctrine of the Atonement* (Edinburgh: Banner of Truth, 2009), 69. Smeaton also argues that the mediator must be divine to fully grasp the infinite debt that mankind owed and the infinite wickedness of our sin. This was necessary for his death to be a willing sacrifice.

So Christ needed to be both God and man to save us. As Proclus, archbishop of Constantinople, said in the fifth century, "Mere man could not save: the naked Godhead could not suffer."[16] Christ therefore became the mediator: "There is one mediator between God and men, the man Christ Jesus" (1 Tim. 2:5). A mediator is usually a go-between. Think of a negotiator in a house sale: the mediator goes back and forth between the seller and the buyer to reach a deal. Or think of a herald going back and forth between two warring kings, trying to negotiate peace.

But Jesus is much more than a go-between. As Herman Bavinck observes, "He does not stand between two parties: he *is* those two parties in his own person."[17] Jesus is able to reconcile God to man because he *is* God and man. In him, humanity and God meet at peace. In Thomas Goodwin's lovely phrase, "Heaven and Earth met and kissed one another."[18]

That is why everything else we explore about the salvation Jesus offers rests on his identity. There is no salvation outside Jesus because only in Jesus do God and man clasp hands in friendship. And therefore, only if we are united to him can we experience the benefits of his work. At the end of the day, salvation is not a gift from Jesus; it is the gift of Jesus. What God gives us is his Son.

---

16 Quoted in Smeaton, *Christ's Doctrine*, 73.
17 Bavinck, *Reformed Dogmatics*, 3:363.
18 Thomas Goodwin, *Of the Knowledge of God the Father*, in *The Works of Thomas Goodwin* (Edinburgh: James Nichol, 1861–1866), 4:439.

PART 2

_____

TO THE FAR COUNTRY

Christ's Humiliation

3

Bearing Shame and Scoffing Rude

The Humiliation of Christ

IF THE WORK OF CHRIST is going to arise naturally from the story the Bible tells, instead of just being a series of proof texts grabbed from here, there, and everywhere, we need to do justice to what have traditionally been called the two states of Christ. These states describe his journey, the trajectory of his rescue mission. They're mapped out in the Old Testament, as Jesus himself summarizes on the road to Emmaus:

> O foolish ones, and slow of heart to believe all that the prophets have spoken! Was it not necessary that the Christ should suffer these things and enter into his glory? (Luke 24:25–26)

"Suffer these things and enter into his glory." Here are the two states of Christ: his humiliation and exaltation. He suffers first, and then he is raised to glory. In greater detail Paul traces the same pattern:

> Have this mind among yourselves, which is yours in Christ Jesus, who, though he was in the form of God, did not count equality with God a thing to be grasped, but emptied himself, by taking the form of a servant, being born in the likeness of men. And being found in human form, he humbled himself by becoming obedient to the point of death, even death on a cross. Therefore God has highly exalted him and bestowed on him the name that is above every name, so that at the name of Jesus every knee should bow, in heaven and on earth and under the earth, and every tongue confess that Jesus Christ is Lord, to the glory of God the Father. (Phil. 2:5–11)

The life story of Christ is shaped like a U. He begins in glory, humbles himself to become man, and ends up as low as you can get: crucified, dead, and buried. But then the curve begins to turn upward. He is raised from the dead, lifted up to heaven, and there enthroned at the right hand of God the Father. And one day, the climax will come as all creation bows before their rightful king.

But we begin with Christ's humiliation: his journey from womb to tomb. Each step is, as it were, a descent further into the depths of humiliation and suffering. We must resist the temptation to leap straight down to the lower steps, and miss the significance of the descent. To do so would be to reduce Christ's life to little more than a warm-up for the main event. No, each step was vital. For us and for our salvation he came *down*.

Step 1: The Incarnation

In the previous chapter, we saw that Jesus is both God and man. That union began in the womb of Mary. As the Holy Spirit hovered over the waters, forming creation, so he "overshadow[ed]" Mary in order that a new creation might begin (Luke 1:35). The Spirit had to create what was lacking from Jesus not having a human father. But Jesus was truly the son of Mary, was of her flesh, and inherited her DNA. Mary was no mere incubator, her womb the test tube carrying a surrogate baby. No, she was the natural mother of Christ, as much as your own mother is to you. The Spirit therefore had to ensure the holiness of the material Mary contributed to the child—she herself being sinful like all humanity.

The virgin birth is miraculous and significant. Jesus not having a human father doesn't explain why he is divine and human: he is not half God and half man, as if God the Father took the place of Joseph. Rather, the conception of Jesus through the power of the Holy Spirit tells us that salvation couldn't come from within humanity but needed to come from above. We couldn't rescue ourselves, dig ourselves out of the pit. God needed to come down. In that sense the miracle is the message: salvation is from the Lord.

In one sense, this first step down brought Christ even lower than Adam. The Dutch theologian Herman Bavinck explains:

> For Adam was created adult at once, but Christ was conceived in Mary's womb and was born as a helpless babe. When Adam came, everything stood ready for him, but when Christ came to earth no one had counted on his coming and there was even

no place for him in the inn. Adam came to rule, and to subject the whole earth to his dominion. Christ came not to be served, but to serve, and give his life as a ransom for many.[1]

Step 2: Christ's Life

After the conception of Christ, his whole life was lived for us and for our salvation. He developed just as a normal child would. Indeed, Benjamin B. Warfield points out that Christ's was

the only strictly normal human development, from birth to manhood, the world has ever seen. For this child is the only child who has ever been born into the world without the fatal entail of sin and the only child that has ever grown into manhood without having his walk and speech marred at every step by the destructive influences of sin and error. . . . It is a great thing for the world to have seen one such instance.[2]

Christ's life can be viewed in two ways: his active and passive obedience.

Active Obedience

Jesus's active obedience is the term given to his fulfilling of the law for us. Ever since Adam fell in the garden, we've needed a

---

1   Herman Bavinck, *The Wonderful Works of God: Instruction in the Christian Religion according to the Reformed Confession* (Glenside, PA: Westminster Seminary Press, 2019), 319.

2   Benjamin B. Warfield, "The Human Development of Jesus," ed. Michael Bremmer, SoundDoctrine.net, accessed 5/29/2020, http://www.sounddoctrine.net/Classic_Sermons/Benjamin%20Warfield/warfield_christchild.htm.

rescuer to do two things: remove our debt of sin and also live the obedient life that Adam (and we in him) failed to live. Someone needs not only to bear the curse but also to fulfill all righteousness. Perhaps the best way into this is to imagine Adam in the garden, before the fall. What was his life meant to look like? What did God require of him? Not simply that he avoid taking the fruit of the tree of the knowledge of good and evil: this was required, of course, but there was more. Imagine if Adam had just sat still, eyes shut, in the center of the garden. Never moving. Never speaking. Silent and inactive. Would he have been obedient? Of course not. God had laid on Adam active duties as well as the restriction of the tree. He was to fill the earth, rule over it, subdue it. Obedience, the path to blessing, has always been active. Holiness is a case not only of avoiding the wrong but also of doing the right.

As the "last Adam," Jesus therefore needed to live this God-honoring, law-fulfilling life that the first Adam failed to live. Jesus wasn't born and sacrificed right away in the manger of Bethlehem. Why wasn't he, if he was already the sinless God-man? Well, he wasn't in part because he had yet to fulfill the law for us. This he did according to his human nature. It is human righteousness that we need credited to our accounts, not angelic, nor even divine. Jesus resisted sin and Satan as a man. Think of his battle in the wilderness with Satan. The whole trial is set up to paint Christ as the better Adam. Like Adam, his temptation was to take food illegitimately: for the first Adam, the fruit from the tree; for the second, turning stones into bread. As he did in Eden, the serpent whispered, "You will not surely die," to Jesus, tempting him to throw himself off the temple, with the suggestion that he would surely cheat death. And as he had done millennia before, Satan promised godlike status for disobedience. Thankfully, the second Adam stood firm.

Passive Obedience

Christ's whole life was one of *active obedience*, right up to his last breath. Even on the cross, under excruciating pain, he had to remain our sinless Savior. Similarly, his entire life is one of *passive obedience*. *Passive* in this sense means not inactive but rather curse bearing. From his birth until his death, Jesus's whole life was lived suffering on our behalf. As question 37 of the Heidelberg Catechism puts it,

> A. During his whole life on earth,
>   but especially at the end,
>   Christ sustained
>   in body and soul
>   the anger of God against the sin of the whole human race.[3]

Clearly, the climax of this curse bearing came at the cross. But it began earlier. On the eighth day of his life, Jesus was circumcised, taking on himself the sign that sin needed to be cut off. The cut in his own flesh was prophetic of the final cutting off to which all circumcisions pointed: the cutting off of the Messiah for his people. It was the first shedding of his sacrificial blood.

And as he grew in wisdom and understanding, so too the enormity of what was ahead of him began to press down with increas-

3   *The Heidelberg Catechism* (Grand Rapids, MI: Faith Alive, 1988), 24.

ing weight. It's astounding to think of Christ as a child learning the Old Testament and beginning to realize how it connected to himself: *The Passover lamb—that's me. The sacrifices of Leviticus—they're pointing to me. The suffering servant of Isaiah 53—it's me.* Again, see the importance of a right understanding of Jesus's two natures. This knowledge of his identity as the Messiah and all it entailed wasn't simply downloaded at birth from his divine to his human nature. In the manger of Bethlehem, Christ could not speak, let alone identify himself as the Messiah. No, as Isaiah prophesied,

> Morning by morning he awakens;
>> he awakens my ear
>> to hear as those who are taught.
> The Lord GOD has opened my ear,
>> and I was not rebellious;
>> I turned not backward. (Isa. 50:4–5)

Day by day, morning by morning, Christ, according to his human nature, learned more of his messianic calling, even as he already knew it in his divine nature.

And before the final suffering of the cross, Christ endured the torment of Gethsemane. The eighteenth-century minister Jonathan Edwards has a stunning sermon on this passage titled "Christ's Agony." In it he argues that at Gethsemane the true horror of the cross was revealed to Christ in all its fullness, so that he would undertake to represent us willingly. The cup that Christ prays to be spared from is the cup of God's wrath, a common image in the Old Testament. In Gethsemane Christ looks, as it were, into the fiery furnace that awaits him. To quote Edwards, "It was not proper that he should plunge himself into it blindfold."[4] No wonder he sweats blood at the thought of what's to come. And what love that he should continue resolute! In fact, Edwards makes an even more incredible observation. In seeing clearly, for the first time, the full extent of God's wrath, Christ therefore sees, too, how terrible our sin must be. God's wrath, the cup of judgment, was not undeserved or disproportionate: God is perfectly just. And so Christ sees, by extension, our terrible wickedness. And yet still he goes! Not only does he show astounding courage to face the day of judgment, but he shows such grace and love that he's willing to do it for his foulest enemies—for you and me.[5]

Step 3: Christ's Death

So central is the cross to our understanding of salvation that we'll have cause to consider it at almost every point of our exploration of the work of Christ. It stands at the heart of his priestly work, cleansing us from sin. It preaches to us of his love and grace, of the justice and mercy of God, and is therefore part of his prophetic work. It's at the cross that Christ conquers sin, death, and Satan, establishing his kingdom. The cross is Christ's pulpit, altar, and throne. That's one of the reasons why theologians have tended to refer to Christ's threefold office, rather than his three offices. Prophet, priest, and king are biblical categories, and each is ascribed to Christ explicitly in Scripture. But ultimately, they

---

4 Jonathan Edwards, "Christ's Agony," in *The Works of Jonathan Edwards* (Peabody, MA: Hendrickson, 2003), 2:868.

5 Edwards, "Christ's Agony," 2:866–77.

merge into one another because he both fulfills and surpasses all that came before him, the true mediator between God and man.

Even just beginning to see the scope of Christ's work on the cross cautions us, too, against taking the categories of humiliation and exaltation too far. Jesus speaks of his death as being "lifted up" and "glorified" (John 3:14; 12:23). To the eyes of this age, the cross looks like the total humiliation of Christ. To the eyes of faith, it is utterly glorious. The pattern of Luke 24 and Philippians 2 remains: Jesus suffers before entering his glory. But that doesn't mean his earthly ministry isn't glorious, when seen rightly.

The significance of the cross will be unpacked in the pages to come, but for now we'll concentrate on what happened. In short, the Son of God died for us. The cross was the place where Christ bore the curse due to his people: death in all its fullness.

Christ experienced physical death, death as we normally mean it. His heart stopped beating, his lungs stopped breathing, his limbs fell limp. Just as with our deaths, Christ's body and soul were separated. We know this because while his body was taken from the cross and buried by Joseph of Arimathea and Nicodemus, his soul went to heaven. Think of his words to the dying thief: "Today you will be with me in paradise" (Luke 23:43). Or his final words to his Father: "Into your hands I commit my spirit" (Luke 23:46).

To say that Christ's body and soul were separated is not the same thing as saying his divine and human natures were separated. No, once that union was made, it was never undone. Christ was, and remains, the God-man. His divine nature is wedded to his human nature right through his death, burial, and resurrection.

God as God is incapable of suffering, let alone dying. This means, if we want to be precise, that Christ died according to his human nature. Don't mishear this: it's not that the "human Jesus died"; there's only one Jesus. Nor is it that the human nature died. Natures don't do anything; only persons do. Jesus's human nature doesn't do anything on its own, separated from his person. It is the Son of God who died, not a mere nature. But he died *according to* his human nature. We see this in Jesus's own words. He tells us, "The bread that I will give for the life of the world is my flesh" (John 6:51). At the Last Supper, he speaks of "my blood of the covenant, which is poured out for many for the forgiveness of sins" (Matt. 26:28). It is body (flesh) and blood that will be given for us. But they are *his* body and blood, the flesh and blood of God the Son. When we injure our foot, we still say, "I am injured." When Jesus dies in his human nature, the Son of God dies. That gives infinite value to his death: Golgotha is the sacrifice not just of a good man but of the God-man.

Step 4: Christ's Burial

Even with the death of Christ, we haven't quite finished his descent. While his soul was received into glory, Christ's body was taken from the cross and buried in a tomb. The one who formed Adam out of the ground was himself returned to that ground. The one who had breathed life into the dust was left breathless and buried under the dust.

There are fascinating links here with the sacrifices of Leviticus, the shadows that prophesied Christ's atoning death. Take the burnt offering of Leviticus 1. After it has been offered, to provide atonement for sins, the remains of the offering are to be taken to a clean place (Lev. 6:11). Have you ever wondered why three of the four Gospel writers bother to tell us that Christ was buried in an unused tomb, one that had never been touched by a dead body before? In Old Testament law, contact with a dead body made something unclean. We are being shown that Jesus's body is being taken to "a clean place," just as the remains of the burnt offering were: he is the true Levitical sacrifice. Even the burial of Christ points to the gospel, the completion of his atoning work. So Louis Berkhof: "His burial, moreover, did not merely serve to prove that Jesus was really dead, but also to remove the terrors of the grave for the redeemed and to sanctify the grave for them."[6]

Death and sleep are closely linked in the Bible. Every time we go to sleep, we entrust ourselves to God, confident that he has the power to raise us again the next day, whether back into this world or safely into the next. Each night, in other words, is practice for our deathbed. So let's close this chapter with the beautiful prayer from the Book of Common Prayer's compline service:

O Lord Jesus Christ, Son of the Living God, who at this evening hour didst rest in the sepulchre, and didst thereby sanctify the grave to be a bed of hope to thy people: make us so to abound in sorrow for our sins, which were the cause of thy passion, that when our bodies lie in the dust, our souls may live with thee: who livest and reignest with the Father and the Holy Spirit, one God world without end. Amen.

---

6   Louis Berkhof, *Systematic Theology* (Edinburgh: Banner of Truth, 1988), 340.

4

"It Is Finished!" Was His Cry

The Humiliation of Christ Our Prophet

"JESUS CAME TO BE OUR SAVIOR. But he came to be our *Teacher* too." That was the opening line of the (otherwise excellent) children's devotional we read as a family this morning. Perhaps I'm being picky, but it seemed to betray a tendency many of us have to downplay the role Jesus's teaching plays in our salvation. Rightly we're concerned not to imply that Jesus was just another religious guru from the ancient world. Rightly we're determined not to present the gospel as if it were a matter of obeying his rules and earning our way to paradise. But until we see Jesus's prophetic work as integral to our salvation, just as much as his priestly (or indeed kingly) work, we'll miss the richness of that salvation. He is not Teacher as well as Savior: he is our Savior *as* Teacher.

Jesus referred to himself as a prophet. In Luke 13:33, he announces that he must go to Jerusalem, "for it cannot be that a prophet should perish away from Jerusalem." Speaking of his preaching ministry, he claims that "the Spirit . . . has anointed me / to proclaim good news to the poor" (Luke 4:18): notice again the anointing, or "Christing," language. The people of Israel had been expecting a great prophet ever since the days of Moses (Deut. 18:15–18). As Peter preaches from the steps of the temple, he links this prophecy directly to Jesus (Acts 3:22–23). Jesus is undoubtedly our prophet. But how does his prophetic work contribute to our salvation?

The Great Gulf

It would be tempting to dive in here and start talking about Jesus's teaching, but we need to take a step further back. As we've already seen, eternal life is all about knowing God: "This is eternal life, that they know you, the only true God, and Jesus Christ whom you have sent" (John 17:3). But before we can know God, two huge problems need solving: our sin and our smallness. We'll return to sin later, but for now let's focus on the problem of our size—particularly the size of our tiny human minds. God in himself is infinite and therefore unfathomable; we are far too small to know and understand him. Just look at some of the ways he describes himself:

Great is our Lord, and abundant in power;
 his understanding is beyond measure. (Ps. 147:5)

Oh, the depth of the riches and wisdom and knowledge of God! How unsearchable are his judgments and how inscrutable his ways! (Rom. 11:33)

Can you find out the deep things of God?
 Can you find out the limit of the Almighty?

It is higher than heaven—what can you do?
　　Deeper than Sheol—what can you know?
Its measure is longer than the earth
　　and broader than the sea. (Job 11:7–9)

Even from this handful of verses, we can see the point: God is far too great for us to comprehend. He is the Creator, and we are but creatures. We are no more capable of understanding the nature and essence of God than the ant that just scuttled across the windowsill has of understanding me. Indeed, the gap between the ant and me is virtually nothing compared to the gap between God and me. As Job says, "Behold, he passes by me, and I see him not; / he moves on, but I do not perceive him" (Job 9:11). Trying to get finite human beings to comprehend, to fully grasp, the nature of God is like trying to pour the Pacific Ocean into an eggcup.

Christ the Bridge

And so we need a mediator. In Jesus Christ, the God-man, we have the perfect mediator, the one who can perfectly reveal God to us. John Owen says that we can think of Christ as image in two ways. First, as the divine Son, he is the "essential image of the Father's person." Son and Father are distinct but share exactly the same character and attributes, because there is only one God, one divine essence. This Son then takes on our flesh and becomes man. Thus he becomes the true "image of God" in a second way, what John Owen calls a "representative image of God to us."[1] What is

---

1　John Owen, *The Person of Christ: Declaring a Glorious Mystery—God and Man* (Fearn, Ross-shire, Scotland: Christian Focus, 2015), 123.

a "representative image"? To put it simply, Owen means that Jesus becomes an image we can see, hear, understand, relate to. The Son of God has come down to our level, speaks our language, using a mouth like ours from a mind like ours. Jesus can therefore say, "Whoever has seen me has seen the Father" (John 14:9). Or as John puts it, "No one has ever seen God; the only God, who is at the Father's side, he has made him known" (John 1:18). It's no surprise, then, that John calls Jesus "the Word" throughout the first chapter of his Gospel. It is fitting that the Son, who is eternally the exact image of the Father, is the one who takes flesh to reveal God to us. Of course, there are some things true of Jesus as man that aren't true of God: Jesus gets tired, needs to eat, can die. We can't reason from this that God in himself gets tired, needs to eat, or can die. But Christ in his human nature is a perfect revelation of God on a human level. This is how we can have certainty that God's character is the character of Christ. We need not fear that there is another hidden God, totally different from Jesus, lacking his grace and mercy.

So Christ, as Herman Bavinck says, "is not a prophet only by the words he speaks but primarily by what he is."[2] Owen goes as far as to say that "a mere external doctrinal revelation of the divine nature and properties, without any exemplification or real representation of them, was not sufficient" for God's purposes.[3] In other words, we couldn't have known God properly if we had only the Bible and not Jesus. The Bible describes the invisible, unfathomable

2   Herman Bavinck, *Reformed Dogmatics*, vol. 3, *Sin and Salvation in Christ*, ed. John Bolt, trans. John Vriend (Grand Rapids, MI: Baker Academic, 2006), 337.

3   Owen, *Person of Christ*, 119.

God using human language, but it doesn't actually bring God to us. If we had only Scripture, we would be left with God's words about God but would be unable to meet him and know him. He would remain hidden. Christ, the God-man, makes this knowing possible. As Owen puts it, "Scripture is built on this foundation, . . . that there is a real representation of the divine nature to us, which it declares and describes."[4] That real representation is Christ, the only one we can go to—one day quite literally—to see God.

The Prophet behind the Prophets

It is always the Son who reveals. He is acting as prophet even before his incarnation. This goes for all his offices, in fact. His mediation doesn't begin at Bethlehem, still less Golgotha. He was appointed mediator in God's eternal plan and has always been the one through whom God speaks to and saves fallen human beings. This is why Peter can say that it was Jesus who was speaking through the Old Testament prophets, speaking indeed of his own ministry of humiliation and exaltation:

> Concerning this salvation, the prophets who prophesied about the grace that was to be yours searched and inquired carefully, inquiring what person or time the Spirit of Christ in them was indicating when he predicted the sufferings of Christ and the subsequent glories. (1 Pet. 1:10–11)

To put it bluntly, this means that the Bible only "works" because of Jesus. He is the ultimate prophet, who knows the Father; is

4   Owen, *Person of Christ*, 119.

the exact imprint of his nature; understands the will, the plan, the counsel of God; and can reveal it perfectly to his people, as he has become one of us.

Divine and Human Knowledge

Christ is therefore mediator according to both natures. Clearly, as God, he is omniscient, all-knowing. But he is not omniscient in his human nature. At times he learns from Scripture, but he also receives supernatural knowledge. Jesus, in other words, not only gives revelation but lives by it. There is legitimate debate over how exactly Jesus receives this knowledge into his human mind. For some (like Owen), it came through the Holy Spirit. For others, there was direct communication between Jesus's divine and human natures. Somehow we need to protect the unity of his person and the distinction of his two natures.

However this revelation came to him, it shows that Jesus wasn't omniscient according to his human nature during his earthly ministry: an omniscient mind wouldn't need revelation. We see this limit to his human knowledge when he is surprised by things (Matt. 8:10; Luke 8:45) or doesn't know the date of his return (Mark 13:32). Of course, at the same time, according to his divine nature he was omniscient, knew all things, and was surprised by nothing.

There's great mystery here. Part of the mystery is found in realizing that when we say that Jesus is one person, we're not speaking about one "psychological center"—as if the Son of God replaced the human mind in Jesus, the old heresy of Apollinarianism. As Mark Jones says,

> The hypostatic union of two natures in one person does not require a single psychological center, as if the "mind" of the

Son assumed a human body only. We may be used to making the personal synonymous with the psychological. . . . So by assuming a human nature he assumed a human body and soul with a distinct psychology that must not be equated with God's own self-consciousness.[5]

Jesus had—and has—a real human mind, dependent on revelation. In fact, his human mind is not omniscient even now in glory; if it were, it would no longer be truly human. Yet as a glorified *man*, far more has been revealed to him (Rev. 22:12), and his human mind is as great as is possible, while remaining just that: human.

Christ the Preacher

Everything Christ did, therefore, revealed God to us. But we need to pay special attention to his words. Without them, his saving acts become incomprehensible to us.

Recently, American football and particularly the Super Bowl have begun to feature more prominently on British TV. Almost no one plays the sport over here, and so when it comes on the screen, the temptation is to dismiss it as simply an inferior version of rugby. Why has it grown in popularity? Because of the commentary. Slowly the experts who understand the action have taught a new audience what is going on—and why. The eye alone couldn't comprehend: the ear is the secret to success.

Were we to have stood on a hill overlooking Jerusalem some two thousand years ago, little would have suggested that we were

---

5 Mark Jones, *A Christian's Pocket Guide to Jesus Christ: An Introduction to Christology* (Fearn, Ross-shire, Scotland: Christian Focus, 2012), 11.

looking at the crucifixion of the Son of God. The skies darkened, the temple curtain ripped (not that we would have seen that), but none of these things in and of themselves provided an explanation of what was going on and why. The eye would have been useless unless the ear had already heard. Jesus, prophetically through the Old Testament, and then in his own preaching ministry, had explained that he had come to give his life "as a ransom for many" (Mark 10:45). It is his explanation of the cross to which we must cling. As we'll see, he continues to speak through the apostles and prophets after he ascends to glory. And these words are life-giving.

Jesus demonstrates this in many of his miraculous healings. Were he a mere man, his words could seem cruel. What sort of person tells a paralytic to stand up? A blind man to look? Who goes with a weeping woman to the fresh grave of her brother and then commands the corpse to come out? Only someone whose word has the power to bring about the response to its command. Jesus's word is never mere information: it is the very word of God, a word so powerful it spoke the universe into being, a word that always achieves its end. Jesus's word is powerful to save, to bring the life won at the cross to spiritually dead men and women.

The Cross as Pulpit

How that life-giving word comes to us will have to wait. We live, after all, in the age of Christ's exaltation, and our attention for now is on his humiliation. Before we move on, we need to return once more to the cross. The cross is not just about Christ's priestly work; it also stands at the heart of his prophetic ministry. The cross preaches to us. The cross is Christ's pulpit.

Of course, the cross preaches to us of the love and justice of God and of the unflinching desire of Jesus to save us. We'll speak more of this in the following chapter. Here let's focus on how at the cross Christ sets us an example, laying down his life that we might live. Although our lives and deaths obviously don't atone for sin as his does, his death is still a pattern for us. We are to take up our cross and follow him, suffering and laying down our lives for his sake and in love for our neighbors. This is a major theme of 1 Peter. The apostle encourages Christians to endure suffering and remain godly, however unjustly they are treated. Why? "For to this you have been called, because Christ also suffered for you, leaving you an example, so that you might follow in his steps" (1 Pet. 2:21).

In fact, the cross is meant to completely reshape how we see the world. No one saw this more clearly than Martin Luther. He spoke often of the difference between theologians of glory and theologians of the cross. Theologians of glory still think and work in worldly terms. God is to be found in might and majesty, power and glory. Theologians of the cross realize that when God was acting most powerfully in history, all one would have seen was a naked Jewish man being crucified on a hill outside a relatively unimportant provincial city. There was no outward glory, no angel choir, no triumphant display. Yet that cross was the ultimate revelation of the power and wisdom of God. The cross teaches us not to think as human wisdom teaches. A theologian of glory might reason that because God is great and mighty, the way to heaven must be to become great and mighty too, lording it over others. The theologian of the cross understands that greatness in this kingdom is found in humility and service.

This has much to say to our understanding of church. Theologians of glory will naturally want a church that impresses the world: beautiful people, ideally a sprinkling of celebrities, worship styled after whatever happens to be "hot" right now, a preacher and sermon that fit hand in glove with contemporary culture—funny, chatty, nonconfrontational, nondogmatic. Theologians of the cross are content to trust God's upside-down means: they know that the power and wisdom of God are found through the preaching of Christ crucified. They know that not many of them look impressive in worldly terms:

> But God chose what is foolish in the world to shame the wise; God chose what is weak in the world to shame the strong; God chose what is low and despised in the world, even things that are not, to bring to nothing things that are, so that no human being might boast in the presence of God. (1 Cor. 1:27–29)

They know that the message, the messengers, and the method (preaching) all seem foolish and weak. But they know this too: Jesus also looked utterly foolish, utterly defeated as he hung dying at Calvary. Yet in that death was the power and glory to transform the universe. The cross is Christ's pulpit.

5

In My Place Condemned
He Stood

The Humiliation of Christ Our Priest

MORE THAN ANY OTHER New Testament book, Hebrews focuses our attention on Jesus as priest. The writer (whoever he may be) is keen to persuade his readers not to go back to the shadows and symbols of the Old Testament but instead to embrace Jesus, the one to whom the shadows pointed. These early Jewish Christians would have been familiar with the anointed high priest. Beginning with Aaron, there was a long line of men "messiahed" as the chief representative of Israel before God (Lev. 8:12). The high priest would wear a breastplate containing twelve gemstones, one for each of the tribes of Israel, as well as two onyx stones on his shoulders engraved in the same way. Once a year he would appear before the Lord in the Most Holy Place, symbolically carrying the people into God's presence (Ex. 28:6–21). Thus, the stage was set for Jesus to come and fulfill the picture, bearing his people on his shoulders into the very halls of heaven.

Hebrews 5:1 gives us the classic New Testament definition of a high priest:

> For every high priest chosen from among men is appointed to act on behalf of men in relation to God, to offer gifts and sacrifices for sins.

Three elements make up Christ's priesthood: he must be human to represent us, he must offer a sacrifice for sin, and his priestly work must be directed primarily toward God. Let's take these three in reverse order and see how they shape Christ's priestly work.

Was the Cross Necessary?

Let's start with the phrase "in relation to God" (Heb. 5:1). Crucial to a right understanding of the cross is realizing that it is God who needs reconciling to mankind, far more than mankind to God. True, we are hostile to him, fleeing his presence and suppressing the truth embedded within us. It will take a miracle to turn us around. But no change of heart on our behalf would be possible or effective, without the far greater work of making it possible for God to be favorable toward us.

Already we need to be careful. I'm not suggesting that God the Father was hostile to us until God the Son twisted his arm into being merciful. Nor am I saying that the cross makes God love us. Rather, it is because the Father loves us that he sends his Son to the cross. After all, the Bible's most famous verse tells us, "God so loved the world that he gave his only Son" (John 3:16). As John Stott puts it, "God's love is the source, not the consequence, of the atonement."[1]

---

1   John Stott, *The Cross of Christ* (Leicester, UK: Inter-Varsity Press, 2004), 174.

Yet this love doesn't get rid of the need for the cross. In this sense the death of Christ is necessary. Again, we tread carefully. We must protect both the grace and justice of God. Once humans had fallen into sin, God was not obliged to forgive us. The gospel is an undeserved gift, and in this way the cross was not at all necessary. But once God had decided to forgive, the sacrifice of Christ became necessary. Sin deserves death, as we are reminded time and again in Scripture. God is rightfully angry at our rebellion, and indeed, he would not be just if he were not angry at our sin. So for God and man to be reconciled, the death penalty needs to be paid.

Offended by the Bible's teaching on sin, wrath, and judgment, many have tried to portray the cross as "subjective," its primary work being aimed toward us, not God. We have no space to examine all these "theories" now, but the general idea is that the cross is meant to inspire us in some way. Perhaps we realize the damaging effects of sin by seeing the horror of the crucifixion. Perhaps we're driven to live more sacrificial lives in imitation of Christ. You get the idea. Jesus becomes little more than a role model, rather like your grandfather teaching you to give up your seat on the train or hold the door open for your sister. These theories all have elements of truth, of course, but they make no sense when detached from an understanding of Christ's death as a sacrifice offered to God. They have their place and help show how the cross is also part of Christ's prophetic work, setting us an example (1 Pet. 3:14–18). But they must not be used to undermine his priestly work, that of offering a sacrifice for sin "in relation to God," to return to the language of Hebrews 5:1.

Jesus's priestly death on the cross is therefore an objective work before it is subjective. It deals with the righteous anger of a holy

God, pays the righteous penalty of a just God. In Hugh Martin's words, "It propitiates God; it intercedes to God. It satisfies God's justice; it pacifies God's wrath; it secures God's favour; it seals God's covenant love; and gives effect to God's eternal purpose and grace."[2]

What Did the Cross Achieve?

Most Christians can tell you that Christ died for them. Ask why, and perhaps you'll receive the answer "For our sin." This brings us to our second phrase from Hebrews 5:1, where the high priest "offer[s] gifts and sacrifices for sin." Yet the Bible dives deeper, revealing to us why sin required a sacrifice, why Christ's love resulted in death. The *why* matters. C. S. Lewis has been an unhelpful guide here. In his classic *Mere Christianity*, he argues that once we believe Christ died to save us, it doesn't matter how we understand this salvation:

> The central belief is that Christ's death has somehow put us right with God and given us a fresh start. Theories as to how it did this are another matter. . . . [A]ny theories we build up as to how Christ's death did all this are, in my view, quite secondary.[3]

There is certainly mystery to the atonement, as we'll see. But the Bible has much to say on the question of how Jesus saves; it doesn't just leave us with the bare fact that he saves.

2 Hugh Martin, *The Atonement: In Its Relations to the Covenant, the Priesthood, the Intercession of Our Lord* (Edinburgh: Banner of Truth, 2013), 38.

3 C. S. Lewis, *Mere Christianity* (London: HarperCollins, 2002), 55–56.

First, it draws our attention to the horror of our sin. In the simplest terms, we are told that "Christ died for our sins" (1 Cor. 15:3). What is the problem with sin? It's not just that it messes up our lives, damages us, or stops us from being "the best version of ourselves." Even more significantly, it ruptures our relationship with God. John Stott points to five pictures in the Bible that "illustrate the utter incompatibility of divine holiness and human sin. Height and distance, light, fire and vomiting all say that God cannot be in the presence of sin, and that if it approaches him too closely it is repudiated or consumed."[4]

God and sin do not mix. His holiness is such that he must respond to our wickedness with holy anger. God is terrifyingly just.

The justice of God is undeniable. Lest we be tempted to dismiss Stott's five images, the just consequences of sin are made crystal clear for us elsewhere in the Bible. Sin in Scripture leads to death, to wrath, and to hell.

First, sin leads to death. This is almost the first thing that Adam learned in the garden as God warned him of the consequences of eating from the tree of the knowledge of good and evil: "In the day you eat of it you shall surely die" (Gen. 2:17). Right from Eden, we've known that "the wages of sin is death" (Rom. 6:23).

Second, death is far more than ceasing to breathe. To die is to fall under the curse of God, under his wrath. Because this truth is so often denied, let me list just a handful of verses:

Whoever believes in the Son has eternal life; whoever does not obey the Son shall not see life, but the wrath of God remains on him. (John 3:36)

---

4 Stott, *Cross of Christ*, 108.

But for those who are self-seeking and do not obey the truth, but obey unrighteousness, there will be wrath and fury. (Rom. 2:8)

[We] were by nature children of wrath. (Eph. 2:3)

Sin leads to facing God's wrath.

Third, this wrath will ultimately be worked out in the casting of God's enemies into hell. As is often observed, no one spoke more about hell than Jesus:

Whoever says, "You fool!" will be liable to the hell of fire. (Matt. 5:22)

But I will warn you whom to fear: fear him who, after he has killed, has authority to cast into hell. (Luke 12:5)

The word Jesus uses for hell here is *Gehenna*. Gehenna was the name for a valley outside Jerusalem, once a place of idol worship, and in Jesus's day was a dumping ground for all sorts of unclean bodies, animal and human. This has led some to claim that the rubbish dump was all Jesus was referring to, rather than hell as traditionally understood. On this view the wicked simply cease to exist at their death. But this makes no sense of the warning of Luke 12: Why should we be bothered about God casting our bodies onto a rubbish dump *after* he has killed us if we then no longer exist? Nor does it do justice to Jesus's famous parable of the rich man and Lazarus, in which the spiteful rich man is described as being in "torment" after his death (Luke 16:23, 28). Elsewhere, Christ parallels heaven and hell: "[The wicked] will go away into eternal punishment, but the righteous into eternal life" (Matt. 25:46). If heaven is eternal, so is hell.

We could multiply examples from John, Jude, and Peter. But hopefully the point is clear. Sin leads to death, wrath, and hell. It is these curses that Christ came to bear. Before we see just how he did this, we need to look at Christ's final qualification to be our high priest: that he was "chosen from among men" and "is appointed to act on behalf of men" (Heb. 5:1).

Were You There?

In previous chapters we've already thought about how Christ is both God and man. Now we can see how vital this is to the cross. When we ask the question "Who died for us?" the answer is "God the Son." The sacrifice is of infinite value. Christ's person gives unlimited worth to his death. No mere man could have paid our debt. It's also only because Christ is God that he can sustain his human nature in bearing the wrath of God.

And yet, strange as it may seem, not even a "mere God"— if you'll pardon the phrase—could pay our debt. As we've seen, Christ had to become man to be our representative and our substitute. These are distinct, if related, terms. Simon Gathercole illustrates by way of the old spiritual "Were You There When They Crucified My Lord?" The answer, he points out, is both yes and no.[5]

When we consider Jesus our substitute, the answer is no. He dies instead of us, in our place. Paul tells us that "Christ died for

---

5 Simon Gathercole, *Defending Substitution: An Essay on Atonement in Paul*, Acadia Studies in Bible and Theology (Grand Rapids, MI: Baker Academic, 2015), 13.

our sins" (1 Cor. 15:3) and that "Christ died for us" (Rom. 5:8). He dies, we don't. At the end of Charles Dickens's masterpiece *A Tale of Two Cities*, the hero, Sydney Carton, swaps clothes with his rival, Charles Darnay, who is awaiting execution. Carton goes to the guillotine, and Darnay goes free. Carton has become Darnay's substitute. So Christ willingly swaps places with us. In Luther's powerful illustration, it's as if the Father says to Christ,

> Be Peter the denier; Paul the persecutor, blasphemer, and assaulter; David the adulterer; the sinner who ate the apple in Paradise; the thief on the cross. In short, be the person of all men, the one who has committed the sins of all men. And see to it that you pay and make satisfaction for them.[6]

But in another sense we can answer, "Yes, we were there." Christ is not just our substitute but our representative. As he died, we died, in union with him. Paul is able to say that "we have died with Christ" (Rom. 6:8) and that in the death of Christ "all have died" (2 Cor. 5:14). Mysteriously, it was as if we hung with Christ on the cross, punished in him. This helps explain the justice of the cross: it is because we are united to Christ that he could justly bear and pay for our sin.

So on the cross, Christ bore the righteous anger of God at our sin. This is clear from the logic of the gospel, laid out above. John spells it out: "He is the propitiation for our sins" (1 John 2:2). To propitiate means to turn aside God's anger that he might become propitious, or favorable, to us.

---

6 Quoted in Gathercole, *Defending Substitution*, 16.

As he died, Christ came under the curse that was rightfully ours. This understanding is sometimes called *penal substitution*: *penal* because Christ bears our penalty, and *substitution* because he does so in our place, instead of us.

The Cry of Dereliction

As the ninth hour approached, Jesus cried out, "My God, my God, why have you forsaken me?" (Matt. 27:46). This cry of dereliction, as it has come to be known, has led to all sorts of wild theories about what exactly is going on in Christ's death. What did it mean for Christ to be "forsaken"?

The Trinity Broken?

At one extreme are those who speak of the Trinity being torn apart. This line of thought was almost entirely unheard of until the twentieth century and the work of Jürgen Moltmann, who sought to find a suffering God as the answer to the horrendous suffering of World War II. For Moltmann, Jesus being forsaken by his Father meant that there was "enmity between God and God, . . . enmity to the utmost degree." The Trinity is torn apart. Not only did Father and Son become enemies, but the Father suffered alongside the Son, albeit in a different manner: "The Fatherlessness of the Son is matched by the Sonlessness of the Father, and if God has constituted himself as the Father of Jesus Christ, then he also suffers the death of his Fatherhood in the death of his Son."[7]

---

7   For these quotes and an effective riposte, see chap. 1 of Thomas H. McCall, *Forsaken: The Trinity and the Cross, and Why It Matters* (Downers Grove, IL: IVP Academic, 2012).

This cannot be right. God is immortal and unchanging, existing beyond the realm of time and space. In no way can the Son be torn out of the Trinity during the events of Calvary. God is one; the Son and Father share one essence. How can they be ripped apart? Nor should we speak of the Father suffering at the cross, even suffering loss. Jesus the Son suffers according to his human nature, not his divine, as God cannot suffer (a belief held in common by Anglicans, Presbyterians, and Reformed Baptists alike).[8] There is no pain for the Father at the cross, and the suffering of the Son is in his human nature, not his divine.[9]

Losing the Love?

Others have explained the forsakenness as the Father ceasing for a while to love his Son, becoming angry with him instead. The strong form of this theory, where the Father is angry at the Son in his divine nature, suffers the same problems as the "broken Trinity" view above. A softer form suggests that the Father stopped loving Jesus but only in his human nature. This is still decidedly unhelpful. The cross is the high point of Christ's work. Jesus himself says that the reason the Father loves him is that he will

8   See art. 1 of the Thirty-Nine Articles, chap. 2.1 of the Westminster Confession of Faith, and chap. 2.1 of the 1689 Baptist Confession of Faith. To defend the impassibility of God—that he cannot suffer—is beyond the scope of this book. All I can do is point out that it is a belief held almost universally by the Christian church until the twentieth century and recommend Matthew Barrett, *None Greater: The Undomesticated Attributes of God* (Grand Rapids, MI: Baker, 2019), as an introduction to the classic doctrine of God.

9   Remember, as we saw in chapter 2, that it is the *person* who acts *in* a nature. Natures themselves don't do anything. Hence we say that Christ suffered in his human nature, but we shouldn't say that Christ's human nature suffered.

lay down his life (John 10:17), and he notes that even when the disciples abandon him, he will not be alone, for the Father is with him (John 16:32). Of course, God the Father continues to love and delight in his Son, as Christ triumphs over sin and Satan for the sake of his people.

God's "Dual Attitude"

None of this is to deny that God poured his anger on Christ at the cross. Rather, it is to make sure we don't end up undermining one set of Bible truths (the Trinity and the person of Christ) in our defense of another (propitiation). Arthur Pink speaks of "God's dual attitude toward Christ, the Son of his love, whom he both loved and poured out his wrath upon."[10]

Or here's John Calvin:

> We do not however insinuate that God was ever inimical to him or angry toward him. How could he be angry toward his beloved Son, "in whom his heart reposed"? How could Christ by his intercession appease the Father toward others, if he were himself hateful to God?[11]

Calvin's last line is crucial: if God suddenly hated the Son in his person, ceasing to be pleased with him, then the cross no longer "works." It was a pleasing sacrifice after all. No, the Father continues to love the Son and delight in him.

---

10 Arthur W. Pink, *The Doctrine of Reconciliation* (Lafayette, IN: Sovereign Grace, 2006), 91.

11 John Calvin, *Institutes of the Christian Religion*, ed. John T. McNeill, trans. Ford Lewis Battles, Library of Christian Classics (Louisville: Westminster John Knox, 1960), 517 (2.16.11).

Yet in the very next sentence, Calvin can say that Christ "bore the weight of divine severity, since he was 'stricken and afflicted' by God's hand, and experienced all the signs of a wrathful and avenging God."[12] Is he contradicting himself? No, he's trying to outline the mystery of Golgotha. Christ bore the wrath of God but didn't cease at any point to be the beloved Son. Herman Bavinck quotes Calvin with approval, adding that the cry "must not be understood in the sense that the Father was personally angry with Christ."[13]

The God of Golgotha

But what of "forsaken"? We may now know what it can't mean, but what positively *does* it mean? Within the original context of Psalm 22, the sense is that God is not immediately rescuing David. At the very least, then, we can say that the cry shows that God is not going to save Christ from the cross. Jesus, of course, knows this: his cry is not one of confusion, doubt, or despair. He has, after all, spent most of his ministry explaining that he would die for sin. In fact, part of the reason he quotes the psalm is because he knows how it ends: halfway through the psalm, the tone changes from anguish to joy, as it moves from death to resurrection. Jesus knows that death is not the end for him, that one day he will rise to lead a congregation in worship of God (Ps. 22:22).

Can we go further in understanding the forsakenness? I think so, but we must tread cautiously.

---

12 Calvin, *Institutes*, 517 (2.16.11).

13 Herman Bavinck, *Reformed Dogmatics*, vol. 3, *Sin and Salvation in Christ*, ed. John Bolt, trans. John Vriend (Grand Rapids, MI: Baker Academic, 2006), 389.

The most careful treatment of the cry I've come across is in the writing of the seventeenth-century Swiss-Italian theologian Francis Turretin. Turretin begins by saying that Christ experienced "a most oppressive sense of God's wrath resting upon him on account of our sins."[14] Christ felt the anger of God—of course, according to his human nature, not his divine, and on account of our sin, not his own.

Turretin next clarifies that the "forsaking" was not "absolute, total and eternal." Christ wasn't left *completely* alone by his Father. Rather, the Father, for a short while, suspended Christ's enjoyment of the grace, happiness, and consolation that he normally enjoyed. This was a withdrawal of Christ's vision of the Father's love for him, "his sense of the divine love, intercepted by the sense of the divine wrath and vengeance resting upon him." Immediately, Turretin clarifies that God didn't actually stop loving Jesus. But according to his human nature, Christ's experience of God's wrath at our sin "blocked" his view of the Father's smiling face.

All this, of course, is picture language. Who can really know what it means for the God-man to bear the wrath of God at sin? But Turretin's account is nuanced and helpful, avoiding the twin pitfalls of undermining propitiation or claiming that God somehow ceased to love his Son.

The ablest defenders of penal substitution have always tried to strike this balance. Bavinck quotes the great Bible commentator Franz Delitzsch, who uses similar imagery: "Hidden behind the wrath, as final agent, is love, just as the sun is hidden behind

---

14 For these and the following quotes, see Francis Turretin, *Institutes of Elenctic Theology*, ed. James T. Dennison Jr. (Phillipsburg, NJ: P&R, 1994), 2:354.

thunder clouds."[15] Thomas Goodwin says that "God should never be more angry with his Son than when he was most pleased with him."[16] On similar lines, Pink argues,

> Never was God more "well-pleased" with his beloved Son than when he hung on the cross in obedience to him (Phil. 2:10), yet he withdrew from him every effect or manifestation of his love during those three hours of awful darkness, yea, poured out his wrath upon him as our sin-bearer, so that he exclaimed "Your wrath lies hard upon me, and you have afflicted me with all Your waves" (Ps. 88:7).[17]

We might say that God was angry with Christ not in his person but in his "profession." Christ in his person continued to delight his Father. But Christ was more than a private person: he was the mediator, the one who covenantally carried the sin of his people. Therefore in his "profession" as mediator—the sin bearer—Christ suffered the wrath of God in his human nature, on account of our sin.

The Face of God

This seems to me to do justice to two common Bible phrases. First, the curse is regularly described as one being "cut off," the final fulfillment of which is found in hell, where people are "away from the presence of the Lord" (2 Thess. 1:9). Even this is a meta-

---

15 Bavinck, *Reformed Dogmatics*, 3:370.
16 Thomas Goodwin, *The Works of Thomas Goodwin* (Edinburgh: James Nichol, 1861–1866), 4:275.
17 Pink, *Doctrine of Reconciliation*, 91.

phor, of course. In Revelation we read that those in hell will be "tormented with fire and sulfur in the presence of the holy angels and in the presence of the Lamb" (Rev. 14:10). God is present in hell but present to punish, not to bless. It is the "presence to bless" that those in torment are cut off from.

It's not quite accurate to say that Jesus's experience was exactly that of those in hell: after all, he knew the torment would end, and he continued rightly to know that he was the beloved Son of the Father, neither of which is true of the lost. But there is still a relation between what Jesus suffers and what we ought to suffer: he bears our curse. "Forsaken" seems to fit this "cutting off" language.

Then, second, there is the language of God's face. When God's face is turned toward us, we receive blessing:

> The LORD make his face to shine upon you and be gracious
>   to you;
> the LORD lift up his face upon you and give you peace.
>   (Num. 6:25–26)[18]

At other times God threatens to punish his people by turning his face from them (e.g., Deut. 31:17; Ps. 27:9). In Deuteronomy God explicitly links this face turning with his anger and being forsaken: "Then my anger will be kindled against them in that day, and I will forsake them and hide my face from them" (Deut. 31:17).[19]

---

18 Although the main text of the ESV has "countenance" instead of the second use of "face" here, the Hebrew word is the same both times, so it makes sense to translate it the same way, as indeed it is found in the ESV marginal note.

19 See also Isa. 54:8: "In overflowing anger for a moment / I hid my face from you, / but with everlasting love I will have compassion on you." I'm grateful to Jonathan Gibson for pointing me to the various Old Testament uses of God turning his face.

At the cross, then, we can say both that God "has not despised or abhorred / the affliction of the afflicted, / and he has not hidden his face from him" (Ps. 22:24), and that at the same time, Christ's forsakenness means that God *has* turned his face from him, in the sense of withdrawing from Jesus his experience of divine comfort as God pours out his wrath. The forsakenness is an objective reality as well as a subjective experience felt by Christ.

Perhaps this is the closest we can get to understanding Christ's cry of dereliction. Just as darkness covered the land but the sun didn't cease to shine, so the experience of bearing the covenant curse overwhelmed Jesus in his human nature, clouding his view of his Father's love, steadfast though the latter remained. Both were still united in their unbreakable bond of love. But because of his love for us, the Father, clasping hands with Christ, lowered him into the pit of darkness. Christ, out of love for us, never lost his grip on his Father but consented to be lowered such that he would suffer the full weight of the curse, including losing sight of the smiling face of his Father.

Beyond that, I'm not sure we can go much further. C. S. Lewis may have been wrong to say that we shouldn't be concerned with how Christ's death put us right with God. But that's not to say that we don't acknowledge mystery as we meditate on the events of Calvary. There's a temptation to think of the cross as a simple doctrine we get sorted out early in our Christian lives before moving on to the deeper, mysterious topics of predestination or the Trinity. Certainly, you can explain this penal-substitutionary understanding of Jesus's sacrifice to a child. Yet there remain depths to the cross that can fuel our wonder for millennia to come. As Hugh Martin writes, "The Church flickers in her divine life, and becomes shallow in her divine knowledge, when she thinks she has ascertained all that is implied in the death of Christ."[20]

Divine Substitution

So Christ as priest suffered the penalty of God's just wrath toward sin in our place. His suffering was suffering of soul, not just body. Not that the bodily suffering should be lightly dismissed, perhaps a tendency in my corner of evangelicalism. We are physical beings, and part of the terror of hell will be its physical suffering. Yet Jesus bore the whole curse for us, body and soul.

At the heart of the gospel is the glorious good news of God substituting himself for his people. Let's give John Stott the last word:

> The biblical gospel of atonement is of God satisfying himself by substituting himself for us. The concept of substitution may be said, then, to lie at the heart of both sin and salvation. For the essence of sin is man substituting himself for God, while the essence of salvation is God substituting himself for man. Man asserts himself against God and puts himself where only God deserves to be; God sacrifices himself for man and puts himself where only man deserves to be. Man claims prerogatives which belong to God alone; God accepts penalties which belong to man alone.[21]

20 Hugh Martin, *Christ Victorious: Selected Writings of Hugh Martin*, ed. Matthew J. Hyde and Catherine E. Hyde (Edinburgh: Banner of Truth, 2019), 173.
21 Stott, *Cross of Christ*, 159–60.

6

Ruined Sinners to Reclaim

The Humiliation of Christ Our King

CHRIST CAME TO EARTH TO . . . How would you finish that sentence? Our first instinct is probably to think of his coming in relation to *us*: he came to die for *us*, forgive *us*, bring *us* home to God. Perhaps fresh from thinking about Christ's priestly work, we might think of the Godward direction of his sacrifice: he came to satisfy the Father's justice, propitiate the wrath of God. All true. But we need to look in a third direction to see the full scope of Jesus's mission: he came to conquer our enemies. John puts it like this: "The reason the Son of God appeared was to destroy the works of the devil" (1 John 3:8). The defeat of Satan was integral to the incarnation. Jesus came not just as a prophet to preach and as a priest to sacrifice but also as a king to conquer. Question 26 of the Westminster Shorter Catechism captures Christ's kingly work well:

Q. How does Christ execute the office of a king?

A. Christ executes the office of a king, in subduing us to himself, in ruling and defending us, and in restraining and conquering all his and our enemies.[1]

We'll come back to his work of "ruling and defending us" when we think about Jesus's ongoing kingly work in heaven. For now our focus is on Christ defeating his—and our—enemies. The angels may have sung "Peace on earth" when Christ was born, but it was peace in the aftermath of war, peace bought by bloodshed. The incarnation was an invasion, the beginning of a heavenly incursion to restore harmony by defeating sin, death, and Satan.

War Declared

Man was commissioned in Eden to rule over and subdue the earth. At some point after the "very good" of the sixth day of creation, one of the angelic beings rebelled, declaring war on God and his creation. We're told little of this revolution, but it's clear by Genesis 3 that Satan was out to destroy God's plans. Unable to strike God directly, he switched his attention to God's images, rather as an enemy might attack the king's children if the king himself is too daunting a prospect. But instead of fighting against the serpent and crushing him, Adam and Eve turned to serve him and thus enlisted in his army. Thankfully, God was too kind to let this new diabolic "peace" prevail:

I will put enmity between you and the woman,
and between your offspring and her offspring;

1 Westminster Shorter Catechism, Orthodox Presbyterian Church, https://www.opc .org/sc.html.

he shall bruise your head,
    and you shall bruise his heel. (Gen. 3:15)

Here is both a declaration of war and a promise of victory. From now on a battle would rage between Satan's offspring and the woman's. This is the grace of God at work: he had every right to leave all humanity to suffer the same fate as the devil, their chosen commanding officer. Instead, he ensured that at least some would return to the true king and reenlist in his army. As Jesus makes clear, Satan's children are not literal offspring: there's no Mrs. Satan around giving birth. Rather, they are any humans committed to the devil's project of death and deception (John 8:44; 1 John 3:8–10). This humanity and those belonging to God are in perpetual conflict, as we see immediately worked out in the story of Cain and Abel.

Alongside the declaration of war, though, was a promise of victory. One of Eve's sons would bruise Satan's head. He would deliver the decisive blow that would crush the dragon, though he himself would be injured in the fight. Throughout the Old Testament, we get glimpses of this battle, perhaps most noticeably with David and Goliath. Goliath—whose armor is described as "scale"-like (cf. 1 Sam. 17:5 NIV)—has his head crushed by the seemingly unimpressive shepherd-king-to-be. But no one takes on the great dragon until the great son of Eve comes on stage.

Slaying the Dragon

If Christ came on a "search and rescue" mission for his children, then at the same time, he was on a "search and destroy" mission for Satan. Satan was both a personal enemy of Christ and the one who currently held Christ's people enslaved. The devil's kingdom needed ransacking, his power breaking. Thankfully, one man was strong enough, a true Samson able to overcome our fiercest foe. Early in his ministry, Jesus compared Satan to a strong man: "But no one can enter a strong man's house and plunder his goods, unless he first binds the strong man. Then indeed he may plunder his house" (Mark 3:27). Jesus came to storm the fortress of Satan's kingdom, tie him up, and carry us off to safety. To paraphrase Thomas Goodwin, Christ would have to win the crown before he could wear it.[2]

The Temptations of Christ

But how does this victory come about? The war rages throughout the Gospel narratives. An early battle comes in the temptations. Satan offers Jesus various shortcuts to the kingdom, escape routes from the path of suffering on the cross to win his crown. If Satan can get Christ to sin, the conflict is over.

The temptations are another place where we must carefully handle the relationship between Christ's divine and human natures. James tells us that God cannot be tempted (James 1:13), but the Gospels are clear that Jesus was tempted, and Hebrews tells us that he was tempted in every way (Heb. 4:15). Is Scripture contradictory? No, Christ was tempted but according to his human nature—and not, in his case, from corrupt desires within. Jesus was so pure that he could not desire evil; it's blasphemous to think that Christ even for a second felt the attraction of sexual perversions, for example. So while Christ had natural and right

---

2 Thomas Goodwin, *The Works of Thomas Goodwin* (Grand Rapids, MI: Reformation Heritage Books, 2006), 5:300.

human desires and needs—hunger, thirst, a desire to avoid pain, and so on—his spotless human nature never brought to him the temptations from within that our corrupt hearts churn up daily. He was truly tempted, truly tested, but he never faltered for a second, remaining perfectly holy in thought, word, and deed, even as he hung on the cross.

Could Jesus have sinned? No, he is the Son of God, and God cannot sin. If Christ had sinned, we would be forced to say that the Son of God had sinned, albeit in his human nature. Does this make his resistance a sham? Far from it. In fact, he felt the full weight of the tempter's power in a way we never will, collapsing as we so often do after the briefest resistance. Who faces the tougher challenge: the boxer who goes down after the first punch or the one who takes every blow but never falls? Christ really resisted and did so according to his human nature. Remember, the fact that Jesus is more than just a man doesn't make him less of a man. Bruce Ware uses the illustration of a cross-channel swimmer who swims with a safety boat in reach. Could the swimmer drown? No. But how does he succeed? Not because of the boat but because of the strength of his swimming. This illustration could be pressed too far, but it helps clarify that there's a difference between the questions "Could Christ have sinned?" and "Why didn't he sin?" Because he's the Son of God, he could not sin. But he resisted Satan not according to his divine but according to his Spirit-filled human nature. After all, what we need is human righteousness, not divine.[3]

---

3   Bruce A. Ware, *The Man Christ Jesus: Theological Reflections on the Humanity of Christ* (Wheaton, IL: Crossway, 2013), 82.

But let's return to Hebrews 4:15: "For we do not have a high priest who is unable to sympathize with our weaknesses, but one who in every respect has been tempted as we are, yet without sin." In every respect? Doesn't that tell us that Christ *did* feel the internal pull of sin, just as we do? No, that would be to press the text too far. "In every respect" must not be made to contradict the rest of Hebrews, or indeed the rest of Scripture. Jesus never experienced the temptations James describes when he says that "each person is tempted when he is lured and enticed by his own desire" (James 1:14). Take the seventh commandment: what is sinful is not just the action of committing adultery but the desire to do so, the fantasizing about someone not one's spouse, or the sexual yearning for someone of the same sex or someone underage.[4] Jesus never experienced these corrupt desires, since Jesus never sinned. Another way to put this is to say that "yet without sin" refers not just to the "after" of Christ's temptation but to the "before" and "during" as well.

In fact, the phrase "in every respect" is used earlier in the same book when we are told that Jesus "had to be made like his brothers in every respect" in order to die for us (Heb. 2:17). Does this mean that Jesus was *in every conceivable way* the same as me? No, he wasn't six feet two and English. He wasn't mildly shortsighted. To take the phrase "in every respect" and push it to the limits of its possible meaning reduces these verses to absurdity: Jesus wasn't a woman. Jesus wasn't born with Down syndrome. Jesus wasn't Chinese. Can he save ethnically Chinese women with Down syndrome? Of course! He is like them "in every respect" in that

---

4 This is different, of course, from a single person finding someone eligible attractive. Sexual attraction itself is not necessarily sinful.

he shares their true human nature. So too with temptation: he has really been tempted and has really experienced everything that Satan could throw at him. But we must not project our experiences as corrupted sinners onto Christ, however "tempting" it may seem pastorally.

The battle with Satan raged on throughout Jesus's ministry: he was regularly confronted with evil spirits and drove them from his presence with the power of his word. Again, we see how the offices interpenetrate one another: Christ speaks a powerful word (prophet) that drives out a demon (king) and results in a human restored to cleanness (priest).

But the final defeat of Satan comes at the cross.

Christus Victor

When reading books on the cross, it's common to find various "theories" opposed to one another. Often the penal-substitutionary understanding we explored when considering Christ as our priest is contrasted with a supposedly "classic" understanding, which focuses on Christ conquering Satan. More recently, this theory has come to be known as Christus Victor, or "Christ the Conqueror." But it seems that Paul hasn't been reading much modern theology: he sees no conflict between the two. We're not forced to choose between the cross as the place of propitiation and the place of conquest, the cross as altar and the cross as battlefield. Take these verses from Colossians, where Paul tells us that God has forgiven us:

> . . . by canceling the record of debt that stood against us with its legal demands. This he set aside, nailing it to the cross. He

disarmed the rulers and authorities and put them to open shame, by triumphing over them in him. (Col. 2:14–15)

The rulers and authorities here are not human governments but demonic powers.[5] Where are these evil spirits defeated? At the cross, says Paul. And how? By nailing our record of debt to that same cross and thereby canceling it. Satan's main weapon against us is his power to accuse us, before God, of our guilt, and thereby demand our righteous condemnation. But by offering himself as a sinless substitute, taking our guilt on his shoulders, Christ has disarmed the devil. Our debt has been nailed to the cross and paid, the bills accounted for. Satan is left empty handed, his list of accusations gone. In Christ we therefore no longer stand guilty. We are declared righteous: justified, to use the Bible's word.

Martin Luther is one of the most colorful figures in church history. At times it's hard to work out when he's recounting something that actually happened and when he's exaggerating for effect. On one occasion he tells of waking up to find Satan standing at the foot of his bed, reading out a long list of Luther's sins. Luther is unperturbed. When Satan has finished, Luther says, "Yes, old fellow, I know all about it. And I know some more you have overlooked. Here are a few extra. Put them down."[6] So confident is Luther that Christ has paid for his every sin that he has no fear

---

5 In his parallel letter of Ephesians, Paul says that we "do not wrestle against flesh and blood, but against the rulers, against the authorities, against the cosmic powers over this present darkness, against the spiritual forces of evil in the heavenly places" (Eph. 6:12).

6 For this version, see Roland H. Bainton, *Here I Stand: A Life of Martin Luther* (New York: Abingdon-Cokesbury, 1950), 362.

of Satan; the accusations no longer terrify him. He can admit his guilt—indeed, help Satan out with a few things he missed—and still be confident of salvation. Why? Because he knows that his sin has been imputed to Christ, counted as Christ's—and Christ's righteousness imputed to him.

So Christ took our legal debt to the cross. This is one reason he had to be condemned by a human court. I often used to wonder why the Apostles' Creed mentions Pontius Pilate: he's the only person named other than Mary. Why not Judas or Herod? As so often, the Heidelberg Catechism is there to help:

> Q. 38. Why did he suffer "under Pontius Pilate" as judge?
> A. So that he,
>> though innocent,
>> might be condemned by a civil judge,
>> and so free us from the severe judgment of God,
>>> that was to fall on us.[7]

It wouldn't do for Jesus to be killed by assassination or a lynch mob. He had to be declared legally guilty by a governor appointed by God, as indeed he was by both Pilate and the Sanhedrin. Jew and Gentile combined to condemn him and pass sentence. Yet as Calvin says, "He was acquitted by the same lips that condemned him," Pilate several times asserting Jesus's innocence, before eventually sentencing him to a judicial execution.[8] Through this we

---

7 *The Heidelberg Catechism* (Grand Rapids, MI: Faith Alive, 1988), 24.

8 John Calvin, *Institutes of the Christian Religion*, ed. John T. McNeill, trans. Ford Lewis Battles, Library of Christian Classics (Louisville: Westminster John Knox, 1960), 499 (2.16.5).

are being taught the meaning of Christ's death: the innocent is judged guilty that the guilty may go free.

Satan is therefore rendered powerless. He can no longer accuse and condemn us as the debt is paid. Propitiation and Christus Victor are not enemies but friends. As Sinclair Ferguson puts it,

> A comprehensively biblical exposition of the work of Christ recognises that the atonement, which terminates on God (in propitiation) and on man (in forgiveness), also terminates on Satan (in the destruction of his sway over all believers). And it does this last precisely because it does the first two.[9]

Nor should we distinguish too sharply between Christ's priestly, kingly, and prophetic work when we consider the defeat of Satan. In Revelation we read that

> the great dragon was thrown down, that ancient serpent, who is called the devil and Satan, the deceiver of the whole world—he was thrown down to the earth, and his angels were thrown down with him. And I heard a loud voice in heaven, saying, "Now the salvation and the power and the kingdom of our God and the authority of his Christ have come, for the accuser of our brothers has been thrown down, who accuses them day and night before our God. And they have conquered him by the blood of the Lamb and by the word of their testimony." (Rev. 12:9–11)

---

9 Sinclair B. Ferguson, *Some Pastors and Teachers: Reflecting a Biblical Vision of What Every Minister Is Called to Be* (Edinburgh: Banner of Truth, 2017), 481.

Notice how all the offices appear. As prophet, Christ speaks to and through his people, lifting the Satanic darkness that has kept the world in darkness. As priest, he cleanses them with "the blood of the lamb." And as king, he casts Satan down, instead establishing his own kingdom.

The Last Enemy

One enemy remains for us to consider: death itself, the "last enemy" (1 Cor. 15:26). It might be tempting to think that it's only at the resurrection that Christ conquers death. But the cross is again central. "The sting of death is sin" (1 Cor. 15:56), and by paying for our sin, Christ took away death's claim on us. In many ways his victory over Satan and death are linked. Hebrews tells us that Christ became man in order that "through death he might destroy the one who has the power of death, that is, the devil, and deliver all those who through fear of death were subject to lifelong slavery" (Heb. 2:14–15). Death is the devil's weapon: not that he has been put in charge of it by God but rather that he can demand it as a righteous punishment for our sin. The lawyer may be wicked, but that doesn't make the accusation untrue.

Death and Satan had no claim on Jesus, though, and neither could conquer him. Death did not come for Jesus; Jesus came for death: "For this reason the Father loves me, because I lay down my life that I may take it up again. No one takes it from me, but I lay it down of my own accord" (John 10:17–18). See how Christ is active—it is not that he is killed but that he lays down his life. Death cannot take him, and it has no claim on him since he is free from sin; he voluntarily gives up his life.

At his death Christ's body and soul were torn from one another: that is what death is. His soul went immediately to heaven (Luke 23:46) and his body to the tomb. But both remained united to his divine nature—and indeed to his person. It is Jesus, the Son of God, who was buried, not just an impersonal, leftover corpse. Hugh Martin uses the glorious image of a warrior who in the heat of battle draws his sword from its scabbard. Sword and scabbard may be separated from each other, but both remain united to the warrior. So Christ's soul and body were separated from each other, but both remained united to his divine nature and therefore his person. The Messiah was dead—but alive, in total control of his body and soul.[10] Death did not win. And then on that Sunday, Christ reunited soul and body, both now glorified.

But the victory was already won on Friday. And here we can find great hope for our own deaths. Question 37 of the Westminster Shorter Catechism puts it beautifully:

The souls of believers are at their death made perfect in holiness, and do immediately pass into glory; and their bodies, being still united to Christ, do rest in their graves, till the resurrection.[11]

Believers are united to Jesus. When our souls and bodies are torn apart at death, this union remains: our souls in paradise,

---

10 Hugh Martin, *The Atonement: In Its Relations to the Covenant, the Priesthood, the Intercession of Our Lord* (Edinburgh: Banner of Truth, 2013), 58. See also Martin's remarkable essays on death in *Christ Victorious: Selected Writings of Hugh Martin*, ed. Matthew J. Hyde and Catherine E. Hyde (Edinburgh: Banner of Truth, 2019).

11 Westminster Shorter Catechism, Orthodox Presbyterian Church, https://www.opc .org/sc.html.

our bodies in the grave, separated from one another but neither separated from him. Death lies conquered; Jesus reigns. Six feet of earth is not going to separate even our lifeless corpses from the Son of God.

The preacher Donald G. Barnhouse was driving home with his children from the funeral of his wife and their mother. Understandably, he was at a loss for what to say to them. As they drove, a huge truck went past, its shadow sweeping over them. Barnhouse seized the moment, asking his children which they would prefer: to have the truck run over them or the shadow? The shadow, of course, they replied. So with Christ, said Barnhouse. The truck of death ran over him that we might have to face only the shadow.[12]

The experience of death may still be daunting, but as an enemy, it is defeated. "Thanks be to God, who gives us the victory through our Lord Jesus Christ" (1 Cor. 15:57).

---

12 Related in Timothy Keller, *Walking with God through Pain and Suffering* (New York: Dutton, 2013), 317.

PART 3

TO THE FATHER'S RIGHT HAND

Christ's Exaltation

7

Now in Heaven Exalted High

The Exaltation of Christ

BURYING THE SON OF GOD was never going to end his story. Christ dies on a Friday night, as the Jewish Sabbath begins.[1] He "rests" in the grave on the Sabbath day, then bursts from the tomb on Sunday morning, as a new week, indeed a new age, rises with him. Thus begins his exaltation. If Jesus's humiliation charts his journey from womb to tomb, his exaltation takes us from grave to glory. Again, we'll follow this journey as a series of steps. But as we begin, notice that this transition to glory is a direct reward for Jesus completing his earthly ministry:

> And being found in human form, he humbled himself by becoming obedient to the point of death, even death on a cross. Therefore God has highly exalted him and bestowed on him the name that is above every name. (Phil. 2:8–9)

---

1 The Jewish day ran from evening to morning, beginning at sunset, rather than morning to evening from sunrise.

The key word here is "therefore." Jesus being raised from the dead—and indeed, raised to heaven in glory—isn't simply "what happened next." It is a consequence of his willingness to descend to the depths to rescue his people. In that sense his exaltation is a reward, something he earned. That's why his "name above all names" is "bestowed," or given, by the Father. Didn't Jesus always have supreme authority? As God, yes. But considered as man, the resurrection ushers in a new degree of glory, even for Jesus.

The Resurrection

The resurrection is often treated either for its apologetic value or as proof that the cross "worked." This is, of course, right, as far as it goes. Herman Bavinck calls the resurrection "the 'Amen!' of the Father to the 'It is finished!' of the Son."[2] But there is significance in the resurrection itself, albeit inseparable from the events of Good Friday. As Gavin Ortlund puts it, "The resurrection is not simply proof of the gospel, but part of the gospel."[3]

A Whole New World

First, we should address what happened. The same person who died rises: the Son of God. As with his death, we must think about Jesus rising according to his human nature. He can't rise according to his divine nature for the simple reason that he never died according to it. So the resurrection is the reunion of Christ's soul with his body: both "elements" belong to his human nature and

---

2 Herman Bavinck, *Reformed Dogmatics*, vol. 3, *Sin and Salvation in Christ*, ed. John Bolt, trans. John Vriend (Grand Rapids, MI: Baker Academic, 2006), 442.

3 Gavin Ortlund, "Resurrected as Messiah: The Risen Christ as Prophet, Priest, and King," *Journal of the Evangelical Theological Society* 54, no. 4 (2011): 751.

were torn from one another for three days. But this is a resurrection, not a resuscitation. Christ rises from the grave changed, glorified, with a more majestic body than before. He is now unable to suffer, unable to die, no longer subject to any weaknesses. He has been transformed to be as glorious as is possible, while remaining human. So the resurrection brings new glory, even for Christ. He is the firstborn of the new creation. In that sense Easter Sunday is the New Testament equivalent of Genesis 1:1—God spoke, Christ rose, and the new world sprang to life. Paul calls Jesus's resurrection the "firstfruits" of the harvest (1 Cor. 15:20–23). His case is not so much that "God did this once, so he can do it again," as "Christ is the firstfruits of the one harvest, and our resurrections are certain because they are inseparably linked to Jesus's." There is only one harvest, albeit the first and last fruits are gathered thousands of years apart. In fact, as "the firstborn" of the new creation (Col. 1:15–18), Christ is the guarantee that a whole new cosmos is on its way and has indeed begun. The tomb of Christ was the womb of a whole new world.

The Justification of Christ

There's much we could say on the significance of the resurrection, but as with the cross, that will largely have to wait for later chapters. Before we move on, though, we should note that Paul calls the resurrection Jesus's "vindicat[ion]" (1 Tim. 3:16). It is God's declaration that Christ was innocent and personally undeserving of death, worthy, in fact, of being raised and glorified. Interestingly, the word translated "vindicated" in the ESV is the same word used elsewhere for "justified." Clearly, Jesus didn't need to be justified in the sense we are: counted righteous through faith alone on account of someone else's work. But his "justification" is the basis for ours. We are declared righteous because we are united to him, the truly righteous one. Hence Paul can say that Christ was "delivered up for our trespasses and raised for our justification" (Rom. 4:25). Every blessing we receive by grace alone belongs by rights to Christ first.

The Ascension

For forty days after his resurrection, Christ appeared to his disciples and taught them. But eventually this transitional period came to an end, and it was time for him to ascend to glory. The ascension is recorded in both Acts 1 and Luke 24. Both passages make clear that Christ went up physically to heaven. Wherever heaven may be, it is a created place. Only God is eternal and uncreated, "dwelling" beyond time and space. Christians do not believe in two eternal realities: God and his heavenly home. No, God created heaven in the beginning to be the place where his glory would be shown, enthroned among the angels. To this heaven—now also the dwelling place of those believers who have died in the faith—Christ ascended.

As with the resurrection, the ascension was prophesied and pictured in the Old Testament. Elijah went up to heaven in a whirlwind, chariots and horses of fire carrying him to glory (2 Kings 2). And Psalm 24 gives us the heavenly camera angle on Acts 1, as the king who once ascended the hill of Golgotha now ascends to the Jerusalem above, the gates thrown open for the king of glory.[4]

---

4   I'm grateful to my friend Jake Pickles for this insight.

The Real Absence

A central implication of the ascension is that Jesus is no longer with us: Christians believe in the real absence of Christ. Yes, he dwells in our hearts and is with us, spiritually, to the end of the age. But he is also really absent. It's a reminder that God's plans are not yet complete. The groom and bride are yet to be fully united. This age is meant to be a time of waiting and of yearning: all is not yet right with God's world. Michael Horton warns that if we don't take this "real absence" seriously, if we don't reconcile ourselves to living in the present age as God has ordered it, the church will make the mistake of trying to "bring Jesus down" before his time.[5]

We see this dynamic in the experience of Israel at Sinai. The story has many similarities with Acts 1. Both tell of the leaders of God's people (Moses and Christ, respectively) going up into the clouds, surrounded by fire and rushing wind, initiating a new covenant era. What happens while Moses is "absent"? The people of Israel, unable to wait, start to innovate, creating the golden calf and worshiping it as Yahweh. It's not, notice, that they abandon Yahweh for Baal or Dagon. Rather, in the absence of their leader, they worship the "right" God but in the wrong way. We might say that they break the second commandment above the first. Unwilling to wait and trust God's word, they start making up the rules themselves.

Horton's point is that when we fail to recognize the sense in which Christ is not with us, we fall into the same trap as Israel.

---

5 For this and what follows from Michael Horton, see chap. 1 of Horton, *People and Place: A Covenant Ecclesiology* (Louisville: Westminster John Knox, 2008).

We try to bring Christ down in ways that he hasn't ordained, dissatisfied with the two gifts of his word and sacraments (the Lord's Supper and baptism). Whether it's literally creating and worshiping physical images of God, trying to engineer a direct "experience" of Christ that bypasses his word, invoking other mediators that feel nearer (like Roman Catholic saints), all are illegitimate attempts to make up for the absence of Jesus. Instead, we should embrace the wait, recognize that this is an age in which the church is called to hope, living by faith, not by sight. Blessing and deep intimacy with Christ will come but not until he returns in glory.

I would suggest that even talking about "incarnational ministry" isn't that helpful. The church is not a second incarnation; we are not God become man. Certainly, as we'll see, Christ is active through his church. But the incarnation was a unique event, and we await its climax when Christ and his people are reunited. Until then, we should, like Paul, seek to "become all things to all people, that by all means [we] might save some" (1 Cor. 9:22). But this is not the same as becoming incarnate: we are not adding new natures when we cross cultures, nor "stooping" to those below us. The mission of the church is not to become incarnate but to witness to the one who became incarnate for our salvation.

Spiritual Gifts

So Christ ascends, physically, to heaven. In his great Pentecost sermon, Peter explains one result for the church: "Being therefore exalted at the right hand of God, and having received from the Father the promise of the Holy Spirit, he has poured out this that you yourselves are seeing and hearing" (Acts 2:33).

Part of Christ's reward for completing his earthly ministry is to receive the fullness of the Holy Spirit. Here, of course, we're thinking of Christ according to his human nature. While he has always possessed the Spirit, and indeed has been filled on several previous occasions (Luke 1:35; 3:22; 4:1), it is at his ascension that Christ becomes the ultimate Spirit-filled man. And this Spirit is given to Jesus, says Peter, that Jesus might in turn pour his Spirit on the church. The Spirit comes to us from Christ. Michael Horton draws the right conclusion: "The Spirit is the mediator of, not the surrogate for, Christ's person and work."[6] It is not that Christ leaves the scene and retires to heaven to put his feet up and then the Spirit comes to take up the work. No, Christ continues to work but now does so from heaven through the power of his Spirit.

There are other gifts given. Paul alludes to Psalm 68:18 to explain another consequence of the ascension:

When he ascended on high he led a host of captives,
    and he gave gifts to men. (Eph. 4:8)

The gifts turn out to be people: Christ gives apostles, prophets, evangelists, and pastor-teachers. There's some debate over quite how we're to understand each of these offices. But the larger point is clear: as Christ himself goes up to reign in glory, he gives men to represent him. Quite how this works out we'll explore in a future chapter, but it's worth pausing to notice that the office of pastor (or shepherd) is a gift from Jesus, not a human invention of the church.

---

6   Horton, *People and Place*, 18.

The Session

After he ascends, Christ sits down at the right hand of the Father. This sitting is traditionally known as the "session," from the Latin verb meaning "to sit." Peter speaks of it in the climax of his Pentecost sermon when he makes reference to Psalm 110:

> For David did not ascend into the heavens, but he himself says,
>
> > "The Lord said to my Lord,
> > 'Sit at my right hand,
> > > until I make your enemies your footstool.'"
>
> Let all the house of Israel therefore know for certain that God has made him both Lord and Christ, this Jesus whom you crucified. (Acts 2:34–36)

David wrote Psalm 110, but he can't be either of the "Lords" mentioned in it because he never ascended into heaven. The first Lord, the one doing the speaking, is God. So who is this second Lord, the one whom David calls "My Lord" and whom God invites to sit? Jesus. In England if the queen enters the room, no one sits until she does, and no one sits without her permission. Lowly commoners stand in the presence of greatness. But Christ sits in God's presence as his enemies are crushed beneath him.

It's not that Jesus is inactive. In Revelation we meet him walking among the lampstands, and in Acts he rises to welcome Stephen, the first new covenant martyr, into heaven. But his session reminds us that he's enthroned and that the universe is in his control.

Those who try to live their lives under his lordship are often told they are on the wrong side of history, but nothing could be further from the truth. When we take our stand on moral issues, we do so not as rebels but as loyal subjects. As a child I loved to play in Sherwood Forest, home of the English folk hero Robin Hood. In the popular stories, Robin Hood constantly defies the Sheriff of Nottingham and "King" John. But Robin is no traitor because John is no king. The true king, Richard the Lionheart, is overseas. To this king Robin remains fiercely loyal, whatever it may cost him from the pretenders to the throne.

Christians are heirs to Robin. We may be seen as disloyal to the culture and may at times even need to disobey the earthly authorities. But we do so as loyal subjects, not rebels. Those pushing the sexual revolution, the blurring of gender norms, the "right" to take life in the womb are not progressive but behind the times. A new king already rules, and history is heading toward the day when his power and authority will be made known to all. Christians are ahead of the curve, firmly on the "right side" of history.

The Return

Acts 1:11 records the words of the angels to Jesus's followers: "Why do you stand looking into heaven? This Jesus, who was taken up from you into heaven, will come in the same way as you saw him go into heaven." Just as Jesus departed, so one day he will return to judge the living and the dead. On that day every knee will bow and recognize Christ's kingship. It will be a day of joy and anguish, of agony and ecstasy. For those who've trusted Christ and received his royal pardon, it will be the first day of eternity in the new heavens and new earth. In C. S. Lewis's beautiful ending to the Narnia stories, the children enter this heaven and come to a striking realization:

> All their life in this world and all their adventures in Narnia had only been the cover and the title page: now at last they were beginning Chapter One of the Great Story which no one on earth has read: which goes on for ever: in which every chapter is better than the one before.[7]

So with believers: this earthly life is but "Chapter One" of a never-ending life in paradise.

Of course, hell is not empty. Time and again Jesus warns that those who refuse to come to him in repentance and faith, to accept the free gift of forgiveness and eternal life, will dwell forever in the lake of fire. Nothing could be more important than coming to Christ now as Savior, before you are forced to bow before him as Judge.

Double Vision

As we end our tracing of Christ's journey from heaven to earth and back again, I hope we've seen that there's more to being "gospel-centered" than just thinking about the cross. In this present age, we are to fix our minds on both Christ crucified and Christ risen, Christ in his humiliation and Christ in his exaltation. Perhaps at times, in an understandable desire not to lose sight of the cross, we have urged people to look there alone and have neglected to look also to glory. At its worst, a neglect of Christ's ongoing work can shift the focus to us ministering for Jesus, rather than Jesus ministering to us. Instead of him speaking as prophet, ministry

7   C. S. Lewis, *The Last Battle*, The Chronicles of Narnia, book 7 (London: HarperCollins, 2014), 222.

is about us speaking about him. Instead of him ruling over his church as king, we organize it as we see fit. Instead of meeting with and being led in worship by Christ our exalted priest, we see Sundays as more or less horizontal affairs, in which we meet to encourage one another or learn more about the Bible.

If we've lost this heavenly vision, it's not a uniquely modern problem. Writing at the close of the seventeenth century, Wilhelmus à Brakel counseled his readers,

> It is not sufficient to reflect only upon Christ's humiliation, seeing and beholding in His humiliation the atonement. To reflect only on these matters is the cause of much deadness, unbelief and instability. . . . However, the consideration of Christ's humiliation in conjunction with His exaltation will yield much growth, comfort and strength. That is the beginning of heaven, where the beholding of Christ in His glory will be the eternal joy and occupation of the elect.[8]

Eternal life will consist in beholding the glory of the risen Christ. And eternal life began for you the day you came to know him.

8 Wilhelmus à Brakel, *The Christian's Reasonable Service*, vol. 1, *God, Man, and Christ*, trans. Bartel Elshout, ed. Joel R. Beeke (Grand Rapids, MI: Reformation Heritage Books, 1992), 653.

8

Then Anew This Song We'll Sing

The Exaltation of Christ Our Prophet

I'M WRITING THIS THE TUESDAY before Easter. Sunday is approaching, and this year it will be a strange one, a sad one. We're in the middle of the coronavirus lockdown: there'll be no services, no leaving the house even. One of the technical guys at church has managed to cobble together a system through which I'll be able to preach and stream to YouTube. It won't look slick. People desperately need to hear the hope of eternal life, desperately need to know that Christ has risen. And all we have is an out-of-sync video on a ropy internet connection. Surely Jesus, the exalted king, could have arranged things better than this, right?

I'm not sure what the disciples thought when they first met Jesus risen from the grave. My guess is that once they had recovered from the shock, they thought, "This is it! Finally, everyone will *see* that he's been telling the truth all along. Once they see with their own eyes a man who's come back from the dead, they

115

can't fail to believe!" Which is what makes the story of Luke 24 so surprising—and such good news.

As the account begins, two disciples were walking along the road to Emmaus. Jesus walked toward them, "but their eyes were kept from recognizing him" (Luke 24:16). We needn't get into all the details of their conversation for now. For our purposes the significance is in how Jesus moved them from doubt to faith. They were persuaded not by their eyes but by their ears. Rather than doing the obvious—calling them to look and see that it was really him—Jesus taught them from the Old Testament, explaining that the Messiah would have to die and then rise again. As he sat with them at the table to eat, their eyes were opened, and they realized who he was. How had faith come? It came through the teaching of Scripture and the breaking of bread. The disciples' hearts burned within them as Jesus taught, and the meal, the moment the penny dropped, was reminiscent of the Last Supper. Luke, in fact, uses the same verbs in the same order as he had at the Last Supper: Jesus took bread, gave thanks, broke it, and gave it to them. Christ was showing that from now on he would meet his people not in the flesh but through his word and his appointed signs, the sacraments.[1]

This is great news for the church today. It means we don't need Jesus to appear physically for people to come to faith. He continues to speak to his church as prophet but now does so through

---

1 Although we won't focus on the sacraments here, it's worth noting that they reflect Jesus's threefold office. As signs, they speak to us, reminding and teaching us, reflecting Christ's prophetic office. As king, he uses them to mark out who is in his kingdom (baptism) and who remains in it (Lord's Supper). And as priest, he uses the sacraments to conform us more to his likeness, to change us and strengthen our union with him.

his word and Spirit. Luke tells us that during the forty-day period between his resurrection and ascension, Jesus gave "commands through the Holy Spirit to the apostles whom he had chosen" (Acts 1:2). The significant detail here is "through the Holy Spirit": even when he's physically present, Jesus teaches through the Spirit. As John Murray points out, Jesus is showing how he's going to teach from now on: through the Spirit via the apostles.[2] This is another reminder that the Spirit doesn't replace Jesus but is rather the one through whom Jesus's ministry continues.

Founding Fathers

The Spirit's first role in continuing Jesus's prophetic ministry is to guide the apostles in their teaching. Even in the three years of his earthly ministry, Christ didn't finish teaching the disciples all they needed to know to become the founding fathers of the church: "But the Helper, the Holy Spirit, whom the Father will send in my name, he will teach you all things and bring to your remembrance all that I have said to you" (John 14:26). This promise is primarily to the apostles rather than to us. The Spirit will remind them what Jesus had said when they were together, a time, of course, when we weren't there. And Jesus will reveal to them through the Spirit anything else they need to know. To be an apostle, you therefore had to be appointed by Jesus and have been with him during his earthly ministry (Acts 1:21–22).[3] This

---

2 John Murray, "The Living Saviour," in *Collected Writings of John Murray*, vol. 1, *The Claims of Truth* (Edinburgh: Banner of Truth, 2001), 40–43.

3 Paul was something of an exception here, fulfilling two of the three normal qualifications. On Christ's appointing of Paul as an apostle, see, e.g., Acts 9; Rom. 1:1–6; Gal. 1:1; 1:11–2:10.

is why Matthias was chosen by lot to replace Judas: the idea was to make sure that Jesus in his sovereign control picks his spokesmen (Acts 1:26). It's also why you can't find apostles in this sense today. As has often been said, if you meet someone claiming to be an apostle, the first thing to check is whether that person is two thousand years old.[4]

So these will be the chosen men through whom Jesus continues to speak as prophet. To them is added a group known as prophets. There has been some debate among evangelicals over the status of New Testament prophets. Were they equivalent to their Old Testament namesakes, authoritative spokesmen of Christ? Or were they instead those through whom a less clear form of revelation came, messages that were not necessarily the exact words of Jesus?[5] The details of that debate are beyond our scope for now, but the only time we hear a prophet in action in Acts, he begins his prophecy with "Thus says the Holy Spirit" (Acts 21:11), which seems a pretty clear claim to be speaking the very word of God, echoing the "Thus says the LORD" refrain of the Old Testament.

---

4   As the word *apostle* literally just means "someone who is sent," it is sometimes used in the New Testament to refer to others outside Christ's appointed spokesmen. Epaphroditus is an "apostle" of the church in Philippi, though the word is translated "messenger" in the ESV. This should caution us against jumping to accuse anyone using the title *apostle* of claiming the same status as, say, Peter. Whether it's a helpful term in the modern church is a matter of wisdom.

5   For the "second order prophecy" view, see Wayne Grudem, *The Gift of Prophecy in the New Testament and Today* (Wheaton, IL: Crossway, 2000). For the view that New Testament prophets are the equivalent of those in the Old, see Richard B. Gaffin Jr., *Perspectives on Pentecost: Studies in New Testament Teaching on the Gifts of the Holy Spirit* (Phillipsburg, NJ: Presbyterian and Reformed, 1979). Sinclair Ferguson replies decisively to Grudem in *The Holy Spirit*, Contours of Christian Theology (Downers Grove, IL: InterVarsity Press, 1996), 214–21.

In Ephesians 2:20, Paul tells us that the church is "built on the foundation of the apostles and prophets," and the only material we have that is described as a prophecy in the New Testament is the book of Revelation. This seems to me to imply that prophets in the New Testament, like those in the Old, spoke the very word of God.

That's why the writings of these apostles and prophets form what we call the New Testament. As Jesus's authorized spokesmen, they are like walking, talking bibles. Their writings become Scripture.[6] John describes the book we call Revelation as a prophecy (Rev. 1:3; 22:18–19), Peter identifies Paul's writings as Scripture (2 Pet. 3:16–17), and Paul quotes Luke's Gospel and again calls it Scripture (1 Tim. 5:18). The voice of the apostles and prophets in Scripture is the voice of Christ.

Hearing the Voice

All this helps explain why Jesus has such a high view of Scripture—he wrote it. Of course, it came through the human minds and hands he appointed for the task; rarely do we come across "divine dictation" in the Bible. But still, every word of Scripture, Old Testament and New, comes from Christ the mediator, Christ our prophet. In one sense Jesus never "quotes" the Old Testament; rather, he repeats what he said earlier.

Hence Paul can say that "the Scripture says to Pharaoh, 'For this very purpose I have raised you up,'" when actually it was God talking, not, strictly speaking, Scripture (Rom. 9:17, quoting Ex. 9:16).

---

6 Not necessarily *all* their writings, however, become Scripture. We know that Paul wrote letters now lost, but that doesn't mean the Bible is somehow lacking.

Or Jesus, teaching on the marriage of Adam and Eve, claims that it was God who said, "Therefore a man shall leave his father and mother" (Matt. 19:5), when if we read the text of Genesis 2:24, we would see that it was the narrator. The point each time is the same: what Scripture says, God says. And, as ever, this revelation from God comes through Christ the mediator. New as well as Old Testament prophets are carried by the Spirit of Christ (1 Pet. 1:11).

So Jesus continues to speak to his people through the Bible: Scripture is not just God breathed but God breathing. Hebrews brings this out beautifully. Quoting Psalm 95, the author says,

Therefore, as the Holy Spirit says,

"Today, if you hear his voice . . ." (Heb. 3:7)

Notice that it's not what the Holy Spirit "said" but "says," present tense: the Spirit is still speaking today, still saying Psalm 95. The Bible is a living word. When we come to small group, personal devotions, or the Sunday service, we are listening not just to what Christ said but to what Christ is saying. The Bible is a book not just about him but from him. Or as more than one person has put it, "Want to hear the Holy Spirit's voice? Read the Bible. Want to hear the Holy Spirit's voice audibly? Read it aloud."[7] Perhaps it may help pastorally to speak more often of "what Jesus says" rather than always "what the Bible says," if only to make clear who the encouragement, promise, or indeed command is coming from.

---

7 I'm unsure of the origin of this quotation. I've seen it attributed to John Piper and Justin Peters, among others.

Likewise, many church services introduce readings with "Let us hear the Spirit's voice" or "Listen to what Christ is saying to us today."

Look: Who's Talking?

Once we realize that Christ is still active in his prophetic ministry, it changes how we view sermons too. Most Christians throughout most of history haven't been able to read the Bible for themselves, for the simple reason that they couldn't read and didn't own a Bible. That's why there are hundreds of commands in Scripture to listen to God's word but few, if any, to read it: for most, this would have been an utter impossibility. None of this is to say, of course, that it isn't a very good thing to be reading the Bible if we can. But for most Christians, their spiritual food came—and comes—through the reading and preaching of God's word on Sunday.

For a long time, I tended to think of preaching as someone speaking to others about Jesus. That's true in part. But I'm not sure that it goes far enough. Our Protestant forefathers pushed further, perhaps surprisingly so to our minds:

John Calvin: "When someone goes up into the pulpit . . . it is so that God should speak to us by the mouth of men and should favour us with his presence."[8]

Martin Luther: "Tis a right excellent thing, that every honest pastor's and preacher's mouth is Christ's mouth."[9]

---

8 John Calvin, *Sermons on 1 Timothy*, trans. Robert White (Edinburgh: Banner of Truth, 2018), 337.

9 Quoted in Karl Barth, *Church Dogmatics*, ed. G. W. Bromiley and T. F. Torrance (Edinburgh: T&T Clark, 1936), 1.1:96.

Nehemiah Rogers: "The text is the word of God abridged: preaching is the word of God enlarged."[10]

Heinrich Bullinger, in the Second Helvetic Confession: "The preaching of the word of God is the word of God."[11]

These men were either at the heart of the Reformation or instrumental in transmitting it to later generations. None thought preachers infallible, and all understood that when a preacher misteaches a Bible text, then God is no longer speaking. But still they went further than describing sermons as merely a minister's words about God. In part, they were reflecting on the New Testament's doctrine of preaching, where stress is laid on the activeness of Christ even when it is his ministers speaking. In Ephesians 2:17, for example, we read that Jesus "came and preached peace to you," even though Jesus never visited Ephesus. How did he preach? Through others. And this isn't restricted to apostles, though they, of course, have a foundational and authoritative role very different from modern-day ministers. In Romans 10:14, Paul asks, "How are they to believe in him of whom they have never heard?" But there's no need for the "of" there: as the ESV margin and several other translations have it, the verse can well be translated,

---

10 For this and similar quotations, see Joel R. Beeke and Mark Jones, "Puritan Preaching (1)," chap. 42 in *A Puritan Theology: Doctrine for Life* (Grand Rapids, MI: Reformation Heritage Books, 2012).

11 "The Second Helvetic Confession," chap. 1 in *Reformed Confessions of the 16th and 17th Centuries in English Translation*, vol. 2, *1552–1566*, ed. James Dennison Jr. (Grand Rapids, MI: Reformation Heritage Books, 2010), 811.

"How can they believe in him whom they have not heard?" Christ is doing the speaking.[12]

Whatever we make of Romans 10, the point is ultimately a theological one. We have one teacher, Christ (Matt. 23:8–10). When your pastor says next Sunday, "Friends, please know that God Almighty has sent his Son, Jesus, to die for the sins of his people," is he quoting Scripture? No, not directly. Does that mean you can dismiss it as merely the words of man, not Christ? Of course not. There's a reason that the sermon in your church almost certainly lasts longer than the readings. What is that reason? That the preacher considers himself more important than Christ? Hopefully not. Rather, God's primary appointed means of convincing us, challenging us, and comforting us with the truth of Scripture is through preaching. As Thomas Cartwright puts it, "As the fire stirred giveth more heat, so the Word, as it were blown by preaching, flameth more in the hearers than when it is read."[13] Interestingly, in the midst of his admonition to Timothy to preach God's word, come what may, Paul calls Timothy a "man of God" (1 Tim. 6:11). He's not simply saying that Timothy is

---

12   For a defense of this view of Rom. 10, see Robert Letham, *Systematic Theology* (Wheaton, IL: Crossway, 2019), 653. Letham points to several commentaries that support this reading, including those of John Murray, C. E. B. Cranfield, and Leon Morris.

13   Quoted in Beeke and Jones, *A Puritan Theology*, 684. See also Westminster Larger Catechism, question 155: "How is the Word made effectual to salvation?" Answer: "The Spirit of God maketh the reading, *but especially the preaching of the Word*, an effectual means of enlightening, convincing, and humbling sinners; of driving them out of themselves, and drawing them unto Christ; of conforming them to his image, and subduing them to his will; of strengthening them against temptations and corruptions; of building them up in grace, and establishing their hearts in holiness and comfort through faith unto salvation." Westminster Larger Catechism, Orthodox Presbyterian Church, https://opc.org/lc.html.

godly and male. Rather, "man of God" is an Old Testament term for a prophet. It is not that Timothy is a prophet like Isaiah: he receives no direct revelation from God. But rather, as he preaches the words of Isaiah or Paul, he stands in the prophetic tradition, ensuring that the voice of Christ is still heard.

So next time you're listening to a sermon, try thinking of it not as "Pastor Reuben speaking to me about Jesus" but as "Jesus speaking to me through Pastor Reuben." You are living in the age of the fulfillment of Moses's prophecy that "the Christ must suffer and that, by being the first to rise from the dead, *he* would proclaim light both to our people and to the Gentiles" (Acts 26:23). Who is proclaiming light to you? Christ himself, whether he speaks in English, Spanish, or Mandarin.

Speaking to the Heart

The best teachers know their subject exhaustively. They are clear, too, in their presentation. But think of the teacher who best embodied this at school: even that teacher couldn't ensure a pupil listened and understood. To both perfect knowledge and clear external revelation Jesus adds a final element of his prophetic work: by the power of the Spirit, he enables us to understand his word and receive it with faith. As the light of the world, he is able to shine the beam of truth right into our hearts and bring us to life. The darkness that comes from the ignorance of sin is overcome by the Spirit. In this way we can distinguish between Jesus's external and internal work as a prophet. Distinguish, but not separate—the Spirit uses the "external" word of the gospel that hits our eardrums to bring the mysterious internal change of spiritual life.

Christ's earthly miracles of giving sight and hearing to the blind and deaf—those that best pictured his prophetic ministry—often came through his speaking what would have sounded like very ordinary words. No thunderbolts, just simple speech. So too his heavenly prophetic miracles bring blind men and women to see his glory. The cross sets the pattern: in apparent weakness and foolishness, God was acting most powerfully. Next Sunday's sermon is unlikely to seem radiant with glory. But cloaked in the weak and very human words of the preacher will be the almighty power of the one who spoke the universe into being.

9

Sealed My Pardon with His Blood

The Exaltation of Christ Our Priest

IF ONLY.

If only we had been there during Jesus's earthly ministry. Back in Galilee he seemed so approachable, so kind, so gentle. If only we could have approached him then, even just to touch the hem of his robe. Then we would have felt confident of finding mercy and welcome. But now? Now he sits enthroned in glory, burning with purity and majesty, encircled by angelic creatures. Now he is distant, mighty—unapproachable. Now we fear to draw near. Now we are unsure that the same mercy and welcome await as would have greeted us in Galilee.

If this comes even close to describing your own fears and concerns, then take heart. Christ is as merciful and gentle now as ever he was during his earthly ministry. In fact, if anything, he is *more* so.[1] He is now as full of the Spirit as is possible for a man,

---

1 According to his human nature, of course. In his divine nature he never changes, grows, or develops.

has now been glorified, is now as full of grace as any man could be. The ascension didn't downgrade the compassion of Christ. He remains tender and committed to his people. He remains, too, their great high priest:

> The Lord has sworn
> and will not change his mind,
> "You are a priest forever." (Heb. 7:21, quoting Ps. 110:4)

We'll look at four ways Jesus's ongoing priestly ministry comforts us.

The Presence of Christ

When we thought about Christ's priestly work in his humiliation, we focused on his work of atonement. This work is now complete. The debt has been paid, God's justice has been satisfied, our sin has been atoned for. As Jesus died, he cried out, "It is finished" (John 19:30). The book of Hebrews repeatedly assures us that this paying-for-sin work was a once-and-for-all sacrifice:

> He has no need, like those high priests, to offer sacrifices daily, first for his own sins and then for those of the people, since he did this once for all when he offered up himself. (Heb. 7:27)

> But as it is, he has appeared once for all at the end of the ages to put away sin by the sacrifice of himself. (Heb. 9:26)

Although his atoning work is complete, his priestly work continues: now not about accomplishing redemption but about applying it. He has won every blessing for us; now he will make sure those blessings are poured out from on high.

This, in fact, is what we should expect if we know our Old Testament. The work of the priests in the tabernacle wasn't just to sacrifice. Sacrifice was essential and took place in the courtyard at a bronze altar. But there was a second altar, inside the Holy Place, just outside the entrance to the Most Holy Place. On this gold altar burned incense, tended by the priests. Although the tabernacle was on one level structurally, we should think of it symbolically as a three-story tent. As you move from courtyard to Holy Place to Most Holy Place, you ascend toward God's throne room. The priest sacrificed "down on earth" but also brought the sweet-smelling incense to the door of God's throne room. So too Jesus atoned for sin on earth, but then, as the royal priest, he ascended to God's true palace in heaven to intercede for us. Before we think about the content of that intercession, we can draw comfort from the very fact that Christ is now seated at the right hand of the Father. John puts it like this:

> My little children, I am writing these things to you so that you may not sin. But if anyone does sin, we have an advocate with the Father, Jesus Christ the righteous. He is the propitiation for our sins. (1 John 2:1–2)

When we sin, we need not panic, as if somehow we have "fallen out of grace" or have temporarily lost our salvation. No, we can look up and remember that our representative is in heaven. He has propitiated God's just wrath at our sin, and he need not do so again. His very presence in heaven is proof that we now have peace with God. So there's no need to panic, worrying that we might not have confessed every sin before we die or that we might be hit by the proverbial bus before we've had time to repent of today's sins. No, the propitiatory sacrifice was made once and for all. The fact that Christ now sits at the Father's right hand on our behalf shows that we are secure in him.

This is the theme of the hymn "Before the Throne of God Above." Our "Great High Priest whose name is love" "ever lives and pleads for me."[2] It's not that Jesus has to twist his Father's arm; it was the Father, after all, who gave his Son as an atonement for sin. But Jesus, the Lamb who was slain, is ever before his Father as evidence that sinners like you and me can now "legally" be blessed.

Intercession and atonement are therefore tied to one another. It is because of the atonement that the intercession is not just Jesus asking a favor of his Father, hoping for a positive response. No, he is able to rightfully ask that our sins be forgiven because our debt has been paid. Christ is living proof of our salvation. Those of a former generation used to compare atonement and intercession to creation and providence. Creation and atonement are one-off acts, historically complete. But on the basis of those completed works, the ongoing works of providence (God's sovereign preservation and rule of the universe) and intercession can take place.

In an excellent essay on Christ's intercession, Gavin Ortlund draws this pastoral application:

---

2 Charitie Lees Bancroft, "Before the Throne of God Above" (1863); public domain.

Thus the doctrine of Christ's intercession provides a vantage point by which to see how the grace of God meets particular sins at particular points in time. It doesn't merely cover my life as a whole, leaving the details to work out on their own. Christ meets us again and again in our particular moments of lust, resentment, fear, negligence, coldness—and says, "Father, forgive them, for the sake of my blood."[3]

He ever lives and pleads for me.

The Prayers of Christ

How encouraging is it when people tell you they'll pray for you? Honestly, it depends on who's making the promise. Are they likely to actually pray? Or is it an empty platitude, a bit of "Christianese" intended to bring the conversation to an end? Thankfully, however flaky we may be in prayer, Christ has promised that he will never cease to pray for us:

> Christ Jesus is the one who died—more than that, who was raised—who is at the right hand of God, who indeed is interceding for us. (Rom. 8:34)

> Consequently, he is able to save to the uttermost those who draw near to God through him, since he always lives to make intercession for them. (Heb. 7:25)

---

3 Gavin Ortlund, "'The Voice of His Blood': Christ's Intercession in the Thought of Stephen Charnock," *Themelios* 38, no. 3 (2013), https://themelios.thegospelcoalition.org/article/the-voice-of-his-blood-christs-intercession-in-the-thought-of-stephen-charn/. I am indebted to this article for many of the thoughts in this chapter.

The word translated "intercede" is the same word used by Festus when he tells Agrippa that the Jews "petitioned" him to kill Paul (Acts 25:24). This, ultimately, is what "to intercede" means: it is to ask. Although the nature of his petitions has changed, Christ's heavenly intercessions are a continuation of his earthly prayers.

What is he asking for? For everything we need to be "saved to the uttermost." All the blessings won at Golgotha come to us as a result of Christ's asking the Father. The right to them came through the atonement. The possession of them comes through the intercession. I love Ortlund's phrase when he calls Jesus's intercession "the voice of his blood."[4] The glorified Christ is continually asking that God bless his people and supply everything we need for our journey home. It's as if at the atonement, Christ won the right to a treasure chest of jewels, kept by the Father. The Father then joyfully gives these jewels to Christ's people as and when he is asked.

On at least one occasion, Jesus made a specific promise to the disciples that he would intercede for them. The reason the Holy Spirit was poured out on the church is because Christ kept this promise: "I will ask the Father, and he will give you another Helper, to be with you forever" (John 14:16). Notice that the asking is still in the future when Jesus makes the promise at the Last Supper. The actual asking comes about after his ascension.

Elsewhere we read of the Father inviting Jesus to petition him. In Psalm 2, we eavesdrop on a "conversation" between Father and Son, in which we hear the Father say, "Ask of me, and I will make the nations your heritage" (Ps. 2:8). The Father *commands* Jesus as

4 Ortlund, "The Voice of His Blood."

mediator to ask for a people to be saved. As Mark Jones says, "There is no Christian alive who has not had Christ mention his or her name to the Father. Indeed, if you are a Christian, it is precisely because the Son presented your name to his, and now your, Father."[5]

These prayers are for God's people, not all people. They are not vague, sweeping requests that "everyone be saved" but specific petitions for the church. In his high priestly prayer in John 17, Jesus prays for the disciples and all "those who will believe in me through their word" (John 17:20). He asks that they would be united, sanctified, kept. He states clearly, "I am not praying for the world but for those whom you have given me" (John 17:9). In other words, those the Father has given Jesus and those Jesus prays for are the same set of people. Whoever you think is in one group is also in the other. There is no division between the desire of the Father and the petitions of the Son. These people *will* be united, *will* be sanctified, *will* be kept. Paul makes a similar point in Romans 8:30–34, where he links the predestining will of God, the cross, and the intercession of Jesus together, all as triumphant proofs that God will get his people safely home. Those Jesus pays for, he prays for; the two groups are inseparable. It's not possible that Jesus dies for you and then fails to ask his Father to bring you to life. And Jesus's prayers will not fail.

The comfort to be found is hopefully obvious. Louis Berkhof spells it out:

It is a consoling thought that Christ is praying for us, even when we are negligent in our prayer life; that He is presenting

---

5 Mark Jones, *Knowing Christ* (Carlisle, PA: Banner of Truth, 2015), 179.

to the Father those spiritual needs which were not present to our minds and which we often neglect to include in our prayers; and that He prays for our protection against the dangers of which we are not even conscious, and against the enemies which threaten us, though we do not notice it. He is praying that our faith may not cease, and that we may come out victoriously in the end.[6]

Or more simply, in the words of Robert Murray M'Cheyne, "If I could hear Christ praying for me in the next room, I would not fear a million enemies. Yet distance makes no difference. He is praying for me."[7]

The Praise of Christ

As high priest, Christ is the ultimate worship leader for his people. He rose from the dead, promising God,

> I will tell of your name to my brothers;
>> in the midst of the congregation I will sing your praise.
>> (Heb. 2:12)

Right now, in heaven he leads those who have arrived safely home in praise of God. One day, all his church will join him. But even now, on earth, it is this congregation with which we gather to worship each Sunday. We join by faith. But as Hugh Martin

---

6 Louis Berkhof, *Systematic Theology* (Edinburgh: Banner of Truth, 1988), 403.
7 Quoted in Andrew A. Bonar, *Memoir and Remains of Robert Murray M'Cheyne* (Edinburgh: Banner of Truth, 2012), 236.

says, "Faith's entrance is real. Faith's entrance is not fanciful, but true."[8] Spiritually—mysteriously—we're already there, united as we are to Christ.

So where did your church meet last week? There are two answers. One is "The building on Hill Street." The other, extraordinarily, is "Heaven." And just look who's there:

> You have come to Mount Zion and to the city of the living God, the heavenly Jerusalem, and to innumerable angels in festal gathering, and to the assembly of the firstborn who are enrolled in heaven, and to God, the judge of all, and to the spirits of the righteous made perfect, and to Jesus, the mediator of a new covenant, and to the sprinkled blood that speaks a better word than the blood of Abel. (Heb. 12:22–24)

It may look like a drab church hall, the living room of an ordinary house, or a shack in a shantytown. The preacher may not sparkle, and the piano may be out of tune. But at the same time, you are in the halls of heaven, being led in worship by the Lord Jesus, surrounded by all the saints who went before you and a company of angelic beings whose majesty we can barely imagine.

The Patience of Christ

We can't leave the heavenly priestly ministry of Christ without considering this golden passage:

8 Hugh Martin, *Christ Victorious: Selected Writings of Hugh Martin*, ed. Matthew J. Hyde and Catherine E. Hyde (Edinburgh: Banner of Truth, 2019), 126.

> We do not have a high priest who is unable to sympathize with
> our weaknesses, but one who in every respect has been tempted
> as we are, yet without sin. Let us then with confidence draw
> near to the throne of grace, that we may receive mercy and find
> grace to help in time of need. (Heb. 4:15–16)

Here we are presented with the character of Christ our priest as
the ultimate reason to draw near for grace, whatever needs we may
have. Glorious he is; unapproachable he is not. The seventeenth-
century minister Thomas Goodwin wrote a whole book on these
verses called *The Heart of Christ in Heaven towards Sinners on
Earth*. His aim is to dispel any fears that Christ is somehow less
tender and gentle now than he was on earth. In Goodwin's words,
"Let us feel how his heart beats and his bowels yearn towards us,
even now he is in glory."[9]

Goodwin wants us to feel Christ's love and sympathy. For
Goodwin this sympathy isn't just the kind of "there, there" pat
on the head a child might get from her mother after a tough day
at school. It is a cofeeling—a cosuffering, we might almost say.
Goodwin knows that Christ doesn't suffer in heaven. But there
is an incompleteness to Christ's joy until the church, his bride,
is safely home. After all, the statement in Genesis 2:18 "It is not
good that the man should be alone" was ultimately about Christ

---

9   Thomas Goodwin, *Christ Set Forth; and, The Heart of Christ in Heaven towards Sin-
    ners on Earth* (Fearn, Ross-shire, Scotland: Christian Focus, 2011), 191. "Bowels" in
    the Bible are the seat of what we would call our emotions. For a good summary of
    Goodwin, see Joel R. Beeke and Mark Jones, "Thomas Goodwin on Christ's Beautiful
    Heart," chap. 25 in *A Puritan Theology: Doctrine for Life* (Grand Rapids, MI: Reforma-
    tion Heritage Books, 2012).

and the church, not just Adam and Eve. Those who have been martyred and are now in heaven cry out, "O Sovereign Lord, holy and true, how long before you will judge and avenge our blood on those who dwell on the earth?" (Rev. 6:10). Even in heaven there can be a longing for the final consummation of all things, the return of Christ, and the resurrection of our bodies.

So Christ is "not unable" to sympathize with us. Goodwin observes that the double negative may look clumsy, but it is intended to drive home the point: Christ really cares. This comes as no surprise, he continues. After all, the Father commanded the Son to love his people, and Christ is an obedient Son. In glory this love is only strengthened. Think of the friend you would go to in a crisis, the one who is kind and gentle and understanding. Jesus is more so! And Jesus is able to sympathize with us in every weakness because he, too, has suffered and been tempted. He has walked in our shoes. Certainly, he remembers his own sufferings. But Goodwin pushes further:

> The apostle says, not only that he remembers how (he) himself was tempted with the like infirmities that we are, though that be necessarily supposed, but that he is struck and touched with the feeling of *our* infirmities.[10]

Again, Goodwin wants to press as strongly as he can into Christ's cosympathy, without attributing suffering to Jesus in glory. We're happy to talk about the "wrath of the Lamb" (Rev. 6:16), so why not the sympathy of the Lamb? On earth Christ grieved and pitied

---

10 Goodwin, *Heart of Christ*, 240.

without sin. Now he can pity and sympathize without suffering, because he's no longer frail.

And Jesus's sympathy toward our weaknesses includes our weakness of sin. It is because of sin that we need mercy and grace, after all! Our sin should drive us to Christ, not from him: as Hebrews 5:1 (the verse immediately following the charge to draw near to God with confidence) tells us, priests are appointed precisely to deal with sin. Thus Goodwin can conclude, "Your very sins move him to pity more than anger."[11]

Was Christ merciful and gentle as he ministered in Galilee? Surely. But he is even more so now. "Let us then with confidence draw near to the throne of grace, that we may receive mercy and find grace to help in time of need" (Heb. 4:16). And let us do so knowing that when we find ourselves moved to pray, even that grace has come because Christ has asked his Father to bestow it on us. He will keep interceding for us until we are safely at his side. In this way even our deaths are answers to prayer—specifically Jesus's prayer that "they also, whom you have given me, may be with me where I am" (John 17:24).[12]

11 Goodwin, *Heart of Christ*, 251.

12 Thanks go to Mark Jones for this insight. See Jones, "When a Loved One Goes Home to Jesus," Desiring God, January 3, 2017, https://www.desiringgod.org/articles/when-a-loved-one-goes-home-to-jesus.

10

When He Comes, Our Glorious King

The Exaltation of Christ Our King

WHEN CHRIST ROSE FROM the tomb that first Easter Sunday, a new world rose with him. He was the firstborn of the new creation, the king of the new age. As God, he had always been king, of course, but this was a new type of kingship. Now he inherited the throne abdicated by Adam and filled inadequately by his ancestors from David onward. He became the human king that creation had been waiting for. That's why in the Great Commission, Jesus says that all authority in heaven and earth has been *given* to him. As God, he always had it, but as Messiah, his reign over this new kingdom was just beginning. So while it's right to recognize Jesus as king during his earthly ministry, the resurrection is his coronation (Rom. 1:4). As Elizabeth II became queen on the death of her father in February 1952 but wasn't crowned until June the following year, Christ was king from his incarnation but took his throne at the resurrection. Now for the first time, in the words of

Scottish theologian "Rabbi" John Duncan, "the dust of the earth is on the throne of the majesty on high."[1]

Remember, the resurrection brought a change for Christ, as he rose with a glorified human nature. He was the beginning of the new heavens and new earth promised in Revelation 21. And naturally, he sought a kingdom.

Newton's Comfort

Let's begin not with Christ's right but with his might. Whether we recognize his rule or not, the Bible is crystal clear that Jesus is now sovereign over all creation. God the Father "put all things under his feet and gave him as head over all things to the church" (Eph. 1:22), and because of this, God "left nothing outside his [i.e., Christ's] control" (Heb. 2:8). Jesus is now at the control center of the universe, and nothing happens without his consent. This sovereignty has a purpose: in Ephesians Paul says that God gave Christ "as head over all things *to the church*." In other words, everything outside the church is under Jesus's control for the sake of those inside the church. He runs the universe in order that he might guard, grow, and guide his church. As John Newton says, "How unspeakably blessed to know that all our concerns lie in Hands that bled for us."[2]

Church and Kingdom

Although Jesus rules over all creation, this isn't usually what the Bible means when it speaks about his kingdom. It is possible, after all, to

---

1 Quoted in A. Moody Stuart, *Recollections of the Late John Duncan* (Edinburgh, 1872), 186.

2 This quote comes from an undated manuscript in private ownership. I'm grateful to the owner and the John Newton Project for this information. For more on the latter, see http://www.johnnewton.org/.

be outside the kingdom (Mark 4:11). This can't mean that people are outside Christ's power—they'd need to escape creation to evade his power! Rather, it refers to those who don't willingly submit to his reign. Our focus here is what we might call Christ's authority rather than his power, his right rather than his might. Put simply, those in the kingdom are those who recognize the king, turning and trusting him for the forgiveness of their sins and serving him as Lord. There is therefore a very close relationship between church and kingdom. The two are not totally synonymous: *kingdom* is a broader term than *church*, as you can easily discover by trying to substitute the word *church* for *kingdom* whenever it occurs in the New Testament. The results won't make much sense! But neither can the two be separated. It's impossible, for example, for someone to be in the kingdom and not in the church. In Colossians Paul tells us that God "has delivered us from the domain of darkness and transferred us to the kingdom of his beloved Son, in whom we have redemption, the forgiveness of sins" (Col. 1:13–14). You enter the kingdom when your sins are forgiven, which is also, of course, when you enter the church.

Or take Jesus's words to Peter after the disciple has finally professed that Jesus is the Christ:

> And I tell you, you are Peter, and on this rock I will build my church, and the gates of hell shall not prevail against it. I will give you the keys of the kingdom of heaven, and whatever you bind on earth shall be bound in heaven, and whatever you loose on earth shall be loosed in heaven. (Matt. 16:18–19)

Leaving aside for now the much-debated question of what "this rock" refers to, see how Jesus can move from talking about building his church to giving the keys of the kingdom to Peter in one fell swoop. The keys are all about who is in and who is out of the kingdom. Has Jesus just totally changed topic from announcing that he'll build his church? Not at all: the church is built as people enter the kingdom.

To repeat, this doesn't mean the words are exact synonyms. Especially when it reaches its fulfillment at the second coming, Jesus's kingdom will contain more than just people—the whole new heavens and new earth will be willingly under his rule. But in this age we ought not to think the kingdom has grown if the church hasn't—if men and women haven't come to faith in Christ. Our service to the king will, of course, mean that we care about our neighbor and therefore commit to all sorts of good deeds that serve them and witness to Christ's rule over all of life. I'm not at all advocating a position in which Christians have no concern for human trafficking, racism, or the myriad other evils that bedevil our world. Sometimes you hear ministers speak as if the only thing people should care about is preaching the gospel, as if everything else is arranging deck chairs on the Titanic. I remember a visiting speaker at my theological college telling us he had once heard a fellow minister express his lack of concern about apartheid in South Africa since it wasn't a "gospel issue." This can't be right. But at the same time, we must not think that anyone can enter the kingdom without being born again through the word of the gospel.

Who Rules?

A question remains, though: How does Christ rule over his church? The first and most important thing to establish is just that: it is Christ alone who has authority over his people. The church is not an institution he founded but then passed to others when he ascended to heaven; he continues to rule. All authority in heaven and earth remains with him, and he is active in exercising it. "I will build my church" were his words, not "You will build it for me." So any understanding of church government that doesn't work from the fundamental premise that Jesus is in charge and alone is head of the body has already gone dangerously wrong. Likewise has the approach to church that sees it as a democracy—one member, one vote, with the majority position holding sway. Christ is king and has spoken in his word. The church's job is to listen and submit.

But his heavenly rule is exercised through very earthly vessels. We've already seen that at his ascension Jesus gives gifts to the church of men called to official ministries (Eph. 4:8–12). Evangelicals have disagreed among themselves over just which offices continue to be in place today, as well as how they are to be appointed and arranged. But there should be no disagreement that church offices remain: Paul is concerned to appoint elders in the churches he has planted (Acts 14:23; Titus 1:5). As one friend puts it, "We believe in the priesthood of all believers but not the presbyteriate of all believers."[3]

The Keys of the Kingdom

Another way to put this is that the keys Jesus spoke about in Matthew 16 weren't buried with the apostles. The apostles are

---

3   I'm grateful to Matthew Roberts for this phrase. *Presbyteriate* is another term for *elder*, from the Greek word *presbyteros*, meaning "elder."

unique in their foundational role as the spokesmen of Christ. But the idea of opening and closing the kingdom, of overseeing who is and isn't in the church continues to be the responsibility of their successors. Again, there's debate about who inherits the responsibility. Does the whole church now administer the keys? Is it the duty of the elders? We're not going to try and solve these age-old discussions here. But the keys remain in use.

What are these keys? Here's how the Heidelberg Catechism puts it:

Q. 83. What are the keys of the kingdom?
A. The preaching of the holy gospel
    and Christian discipline toward repentance.
    Both preaching and discipline
        open the kingdom of heaven to believers
        and close it to unbelievers.[4]

Keys open and shut entrances. The writers of the catechism are saying that two things bring people into or throw people out of the church: preaching and church discipline.

It's worth making clear that no evangelical thinks the use of the keys by human leaders *ultimately* determines the makeup of the invisible church—the church as God sees it, made up of all those who are born again and going to heaven. God alone can bring someone into that fellowship. No mere man has final authority to include or exclude someone. The church, too, can both make mistakes and act against God's word. Martin Luther,

---

4   *The Heidelberg Catechism* (Grand Rapids, MI: Faith Alive, 1988), 47.

among others, was excommunicated precisely because he was faithfully teaching the gospel!

This side of heaven, we have to deal with the visible church, those who profess faith (and, as a Presbyterian, I would want to add "and their children"). Sadly, these two groups (those professing faith and those genuinely born again) aren't always the same. So how are people brought into or put out of this visible church? Through gospel preaching and church discipline.

This may sound terribly judgmental, but it's necessary for all sorts of reasons. When someone says that he wants to be baptized because it'll make his gran happy and he'll get a nice check from Aunt Mabel, what do we say? When it comes to appointing or voting on who's going to be the next minister, who gets a vote? Whoever happens to walk through the door that morning? To whom do we give the Lord's Supper? These and many other questions all depend on who we think are members of the church, who has been let in.

Why does the Heidelberg Catechism say that preaching and church discipline make up the keys? Preaching is God's appointed way of opening the door of salvation to all who will come in: we declare that Jesus is Savior and Lord and invite everyone to come into his kingdom. This makes sense: it is the gospel that brings people into the church or declares them to be outside if they refuse to believe. Later in Matthew, Jesus says to the Pharisees that they "shut the kingdom of heaven in people's faces. For you neither enter yourselves nor allow those who would enter to go in" (Matt. 23:13). Did the Pharisees have some sort of magical spiritual power to stop people going to heaven? No, of course not. But their legalistic preaching was "shutting the kingdom," as it denied people the gospel.

So much for preaching, but what about discipline? In Matthew 18, Jesus outlines the steps a church should go through if someone is committing ongoing willful sin. It culminates in this warning: "If he refuses to listen even to the church, let him be to you as a Gentile and a tax collector. Truly, I say to you, whatever you bind on earth shall be bound in heaven, and whatever you loose on earth shall be loosed in heaven" (Matt. 18:17–18).

Notice the language of binding and loosing again, this time in the hands of the church. To loose someone here is to treat her as a Gentile, an outsider who is no longer part of the fellowship. A similar example can be found in 1 Corinthians 5: they are put out of the church. The hope, of course, is that the person will repent and be restored to fellowship, that discipline will lead to the door being reopened.

Jesus's kingdom is not without boundaries and borders. However imperfectly we may do it, the church has been entrusted with watching over them.

That's why Jesus teaches that the church's pronouncements on issues of discipline come with heaven's authority:

> Truly, I say to you, whatever you bind on earth shall be bound in heaven, and whatever you loose on earth shall be loosed in heaven. Again I say to you, if two of you agree on earth about anything they ask, it will be done for them by my Father in heaven. For where two or three are gathered in my name, there am I among them. (Matt. 18:18–20)

As long as we're being faithful to God's word, what we do on earth comes with heaven's stamp of approval. And it's in this context—the context of church discipline—that Jesus gives his famous promise to be with us when we gather. In Matthew 16, Jesus promised that *he* would build his church, even though he would do so through faithful servants preaching the gospel. It is still Jesus who is active, Jesus who is speaking. So here in Matthew 18, it is Jesus who guards and disciplines his church, again through the instruments of his servants.

Most traditions see a central role for the elders here. The authority of elders is sometimes described as "ministerial and declarative." In other words, it is authority in the service of Christ and can be exercised only in line with what he has said: elders can't go around arbitrarily making up rules for the church or refusing to let people into the congregation whom Jesus has admitted. Imagine asking your neighbor's teenage son to babysit your children and giving him strict instructions: he is not to let anyone else in the house but is to let granny back in when she returns from bingo. From then on, the babysitter has authority but only to act in line with your words. If he either refuses entry to granny or grants it to others, he has gone beyond his delegated authority.[5]

Similarly, the scope of the elders' authority is strictly limited. Traditionally in Reformed churches, elders have authority in the realms of doctrine, worship, and church discipline. In other words, they can declare what they believe the Bible to teach, arrange how worship will take place, and oversee church discipline and the sacraments of baptism and the Lord's Supper. But they must go no further.

---

5   Thanks go to Scott Swain for this illustration.

Sphere Sovereignty

So Christ continues to rule his church, both outwardly through church officers and inwardly as he brings men and women to life through his Spirit and word. The church, though, is just one of three fundamental institutions God has established, the others being the state and the family. Each has its appointed authorities under Christ: kings or governors in the case of the state, fathers in the case of the family. The question of how secular rulers are meant to relate to Christ sadly can't be addressed now in any depth here. Suffice it to say, Jesus is "the ruler of kings on earth" (Rev. 1:5), and kings and rulers are warned to "be wise," to "serve the LORD with fear," and to "kiss the Son" (Ps. 2:10–12). The Bible doesn't seem very interested in "principled pluralism" or a supposed "neutral state"—the latter, of course, being an impossibility anyway.[6] Legend has it that King George II stood up for the "Hallelujah Chorus" during its inaugural performance. "King of kings, and Lord of lords," thundered the choir, and George of all men knew that you stand in the presence of royalty.

What we can say here, though, is that each realm must know its place. It is not the role of the church to run the country, seizing political power; she doesn't wield the power of the sword, as the state does. You may find it annoying when church members skip the prayer meeting, but imprisonment or execution really aren't

---

6   For more on Christ as king of the nations, see William Symington, *Messiah the Prince: The Mediatorial Dominion of Jesus Christ* (Pittsburgh: Crown and Covenant, 2012). On how different evangelicals have sought to understand the relationship between Christ and the public square, see Daniel Strange, "Evangelical Public Theology: What on Earth? Why on Earth? How on Earth?," in *A Higher Throne: Evangelicals and Public Theology*, ed. Chris Green (Nottingham, UK: Apollos, 2008).

options. Equally, the state is not to interfere in church, trying to have a say in the appointment of ministers, for instance. Nor, perhaps more pertinently for our day, is the state to take control of the family. Children belong to parents, not to governments. It is up to the parents, not the state, for example, to oversee their children's education. They might decide to use state-provided schools—all well and good. But the government has no right to mandate this. Nor, to complete the circle, should fathers take on themselves the role of elders in the church. They are not to administer the Lord's Supper at home or to baptize their own children at home in the bath—though clearly they have responsibility to pray for and speak of Christ to all under their care.

The End and the Beginning

So we've traced Jesus's journey from humiliation to exaltation, from heaven to earth and back again. All was done out of love for his church. The Son of God lacked nothing before he created us and thus ultimately gains nothing by saving us. Everything was done for his glory but for our benefit, our gain. The whole journey was for the sake of his people. And so, mysteriously, we accompanied him on it, united as head to body. At various points in the New Testament, we are told that Christians have been crucified with Christ, buried with him, raised with him, lifted up to heaven with him, and seated with him in the heavenly realms.

One day, faith that all this is true will be replaced with sight. Until then, we rest on his completed work and fulfill our calling to be faithful servants. This calling echoes the prophet-priest-king pattern of Christ's ministry, as picked up by question 32 of the Heidelberg Catechism:

Q. 32. But why are you called a Christian?

A. Because by faith I am a member of Christ

and so I share in his anointing

I am anointed

to confess his name,

to present myself to him as a living sacrifice of thanks,

to strive with a good conscience against sin and the devil

in this life,

and afterward to reign with Christ

over all creation

for all eternity.[7]

Hallelujah! What a Savior!

---

7   *The Heidelberg Catechism* (1988), 21.

Acknowledgments

IT'S A PLEASURE TO BE ABLE TO thank various people who've played a part in this book coming together. Its genesis lies in an offhand comment from Brian Salter, pastor of Lookout Mountain Presbyterian Church. We had been chatting about Christ-centered preaching and the danger of sermons always drawing to the same predictable conclusion. Brian suggested a more robust understanding of Christ as prophet, priest, and king as one antidote.

What no doubt seemed an obvious solution to him led to an adult Sunday school class at Christ Church Central, Leeds, where I serve as pastor. I'm grateful to the congregation and elders for interaction during the classes and for the time to write it up afterward. In particular, George and Rebecca Barrett and Kate Leach read through early drafts of the book and provided valuable feedback. Thanks, too, to Cate Webster for helping get the first couple of chapters in a fit state to form a proposal. Along the way, Dr. David Barshinger has been a remarkably thorough, thoughtful, and patient editor.

My fellow ministers in the International Presbyterian Church David and Jonathan Gibson, Matthew Roberts, and James

Buchanan have all cast their expert theological eye over most of the material. The book is the better, and I am the wiser, for their input. It seems customary at this point to say that any remaining errors are entirely my responsibility. *Primarily* my responsibility, certainly. But then they did read it . . .

Greatest thanks as ever go to Georgina, my wife, for her patience and forbearance of late nights and endless rereads. Needless to say, my gratitude to her extends a long way beyond her contributions toward a book project.

One final note. The chapter headings come from Philip Bliss's hymn popularly known as "Man of Sorrows." Bliss spent his early years working as a music teacher but became an itinerant evangelist in his mid-thirties on the advice of D. L. Moody. He wrote "Man of Sorrows" in 1875, shortly after this career change. But Bliss would never see his fortieth birthday. On December 29, 1876, a trestle bridge collapsed as the train carrying him and his wife passed over it. Most of the carriages disappeared into the snow-covered Ashtabula River valley below. Bliss himself survived the fall but was last seen heading back into the wreckage to rescue his wife from the flames. Neither body was ever found. I know little else about him. But he sounds like a fine man.

General Index

Scripture Index